Ancient Secrets of Ten Bible Women

Rebekah Binkley Montgomery

M Zion Ridge Press
Books Off the Beaten Path

www.MtZionRidgePress.com

Mt Zion Ridge Press LLC
295 Gum Springs Rd, NW
Georgetown, TN 37366

https://www.mtzionridgepress.com

ISBN 13: 978-1-962862-54-7

Published in the United States of America
Publication Date: January 1, 2025

Copyright: © 2024 Rebekah Binkley Montgomery

Editor-In-Chief: Michelle Levigne
Executive Editor: Tamera Lynn Kraft

Cover art design by Tamera Lynn Kraft
Cover Art Copyright by Mt Zion Ridge Press LLC © 2024

Biblical quotes identified as NIV are from the New International Version of the Bible, copyright © 1973, 1978, 1984, 2011 by Biblica, Inc.

Biblical quotes identified as NKJV are from the New King James Version, copyright © 1982, Thomas Nelson Publishers.

DEDICATION

To the ladies of Pleasant Dale Discovery Class. In spite of my weakness you accepted me. Thank you.

To Lina Wilson who didn't let me give up.

To Ruth Binkley Whatley, who is my sister in all things.

TABLE OF CONTENTS

Introduction

I may have been born under a pew since my earliest memories are of being in church.

In my formative years, my preacher father was pastor of two country churches on a circuit. He insisted we kids go to all the services so we went to church A LOT.

During back-to-back revivals, we objected to attending every night for a month. Dad argued, "How can I expect other people to bring their kids to church if my own children aren't there?

He had a point, but I think we did, too.

I tell you all of that to introduce the narrative style I have used when relating the stories and secrets of these ten Bible women. I heard multiple sermons on them from the pulpit, was taught about them in Sunday school and family devotions, read about them in Bible storybooks until they were more real to me than some of my flesh-and-blood ancestors. These women are my spiritual antecedents.

While the Bible only tells us the barebones of these women, it left me wanting to know more about them.

When I was a teenager and was scaring my parents witless with life choices which I believed were God's leading, I wished I could write a letter to Mary of Nazareth and ask her how her parents reacted when she told them about the visit of the angel. Did her folks believe her? Did they ground her? What finally convinced them she was pregnant with the Messiah?

I wished I could ask the widow of Zarephath how she knew which prophet God called her to feed. I identified with her when my husband and I were in college. We were bombarded with pleas to support worthy missions but we regularly had to ransack the sofa cushions to buy beans and rice for our meals.

Then I went to school in Israel.

I've heard Israel called "the Fifth Gospel." But it is more than that.

Exploring the land, its culture, meeting the people, and studying the Scriptures made these women rise out of the black and white pages, tap me on the shoulder and say, "I was a real woman. I was once flesh and blood just as you are now. I combed my hair, did laundry, got mad, got happy, had periods, was frustrated, felt scared, thought about running away, had good ideas and bad ones, too.

"I didn't know the end of my story when I lived through it any more than you know the end of yours. But hear my story and meet the God who helped me in my hour of need. He comforted me. Gave me courage. Bolstered my confidence in Him.

"Let me remind you again: I was a real woman. I was once flesh and blood just as you are now. The same God who helped me hasn't changed. He does not grow weary."

A few housekeeping notes:

I have placed notations marking "Let's talk about ..." discussion starters throughout each chapter. Look for alphabet letters in parentheses. (A) references the (A) question in the "Let's talk about ..." section at the end of each chapter, and so on.

I went to school in Israel twice and traveled there five times to research this book and many articles. I've tried to stay close to the inerrant scripture narrative. But like every sermon I've ever heard, Sunday school lesson and Bible storybooks of my childhood, I've sprinkled some cultural color on the narrative, painting imaginary pictures, to help us get a clearer picture of the action and the women involved.

Hopefully, you will discover the secrets of God that helped these ten women and will help you to fulfil the purpose for which you were created.

Chapter One
Rahab the Harlot:
Survivor? Or Traitor?

Your enemy is at the door. You could pray, but you know their God is more powerful than all your gods combined. What's more frightening is their God fights for them in ways that defy belief.

What to do? How to survive? How to protect yourself and those whom you love?

Rahab, a prostitute, found a way.

In Hebrew, Rahab means "wide" or "spacious." Her name has unflattering connotations but keep an open mind. By the end of this study, you may come to admire her.

In the story of Rahab, we will discover:

✓ How God sends warnings before visiting judgement.
✓ When to be proactive in a crisis.
✓ How to face your fears and conquer them.

Midday at the Oasis

(I was able to take multiple trips to Israel, and I'm delighted to be able to share some of my personal experiences with you readers throughout this book.)

Although we have just met and a language barrier stands between us, two vivacious, enterprising Bedouin sisters, consummately skilled in the art of hospitality greet me as if we are old friends. They seat me on a stunningly beautiful hand-woven rug and serve mint tea so refreshing I'm tempted to drink a gallon.

They have a story to tell and an amazing can-do attitude. Although they live under a system that penalizes women solely because they are women, the sisters found a way to not just survive but thrive while helping other Bedouin women.

Through an interpreter, one of the sisters tells me, "For thousands of years, a woman was queen of her tent. She schooled her daughters in the art of domesticity. Now the ancient ways are dying. Settled into permanent housing, most Bedouins wander the desert sands no more.

"Women must now work outside the home to have personal value and contribute to the household. Because most Bedouin women can't read or write, few jobs are open to them. Also, Bedouin women are forbidden to have contact with men, so working as a housekeeper or waitress is forbidden."

With the help of female outsiders, these sisters created a unique business providing employment for Bedouin women and making a profit in the process. Using techniques that are thousands of years old, women weave sheep wool into rugs, wall-hangings, and other decorative items sold to interior designers the world over. Their clients pay handsomely for these handmade treasures.

The sisters explain, "Before a woman can weave, her husband and father inspect what we do. When they see she will have no contact with men, they usually give their approval. You can't possibly understand what a sense of worth it gives a Bedouin woman to earn money."

Nevertheless, life remains difficult for women. Husbands may divorce their wives for any reason or no reason. A divorced wife might have temporary custody of very young children, but ultimately, they will be awarded to their father. Then she will have no rights. Nor is her former husband required to financially support a cast-off wife.

I ask, "How does a divorced woman support herself?"

"She may beg on the streets. Or her family may give her money,"

"What if her family will not support her?"

The sisters exchange sorrowful glances. "That is a fate too tragic for words."

Rahab springs to mind. Was selling her body the only way she could survive?

If you lived in an oppressive climate like the one in which Rahab lived, what would you do to support yourself and your family? Or would your life also be too tragic for words?

A Warning from a Wasteland

Jericho was in the metaphorical crosshairs of the Israelite army. Standing like a sentry over Canaan, its defeat was key to victory over the rest of the land. Perched atop a steep plateau and protected by three concentric walls, it promised would-be invaders an uphill battle.

In Rahab's day, Jericho was an oasis surrounded by a tortured landscape.

Once the Jericho plain was lush and well-watered. Then, only five miles from Jericho's walls, God destroyed Sodom and Gomorrah with fire and brimstone.

The Jericho plain has a long memory. It remains destroyed today.

Citizens of Jericho heard frightening rumors of miraculous ways the

Lord God fought for the Israelites at the Red Sea and in other battles. (Read Joshua 2:10) They might initially have discounted reports as rumors or exaggerations; but in a few days, the unconvinced would eat their words when they witnessed water from the Jordan River stack up in a column before their very eyes and see the Israelites crossing the Jordan on dry land—during flood stage! (Read Joshua 3:13-17)

Yes, the famed ex-slaves of Egypt and their mighty God were spread along the Jordan River studying Jericho's walls for any weakness. After all they had heard about the Israelites, Jericho's inhabitants had a golden opportunity to ask the Lord God for mercy.

As Rahab's story unfolds, you may think she's a traitor. Before you condemn her, put on her sandals, and walk around Jericho under the shadow of the Ark of the Covenant. She will explain her decision in her own words.

If, like Rahab, the end of your world is imminent, her secret for survival might save your life and family as it did hers.

A Night to Remember
Joshua, son of Nun, secretly sent two spies from Shittim. "Go, look over the land," he said, "especially Jericho." They went and entered the house of a prostitute named Rahab and stayed there. (Josh. 2:1, NIV)

Rahab didn't know this night would change her life forever.

What she did know was seven, maybe eight miles away, a dangerous army waited beyond the Jordan River, planning to destroy her city, home, business, family, and Rahab herself.

She had heard of the wandering tribe's past victories over the Egyptians. Recently, they obliterated the armies of Sihon and Og, the two giant kings of the Amorites, so thoroughly even Jericho's battlefield experienced soldiers were terrified of them.

"Something inexplicable happens when they go to battle," they whispered to her. "Our hearts are melting in fear to face them. Their God fights for them. What are we against their God?"

"…their God fights for them." Rahab turned the phrase over in her mind. *What will happen to my family and me if their God fights for them? I wish my gods fought for me.*

She heard the Israelites served a God whose image could not be carved into a rock. He was bigger than that. Rahab caught glimpses of Him when she gazed into a starry night sky. Or saw a meadow ablaze with blooms. (Read Psalm 29 and Romans 1:20) He didn't have to make color, fragrance, touch, and taste for people to enjoy. He must have cared about His followers to put these special touches on the world. She wished she was one of them.

As dusk settled over Jericho, the streets remained crowded with citizens and merchants of all ages and all classes preparing for an anticipated blockade. Foodstuffs were being offered for bloated prices with the anticipations of higher costs to come.

With its three concentric walls, Jericho was considered impregnable. But in a siege, starvation was a real possibility. What kept the enemy out, kept people trapped inside, far away from gardens and fields whose crops were used to taunt the walled captives and feed the invaders.

Rahab heard the whispers: "The Israelites have sent spies into the city!"

"How many?"

"I've heard as few as two and as many as twelve. The king's soldiers are looking for them."

On the roof of her house, the pungent odor of drying flax made her eyes water as Rahab covered the stalks to keep the dew from wetting them. The quicker the flax dried, the sooner the smell would evaporate.

Then, from the rooftop vantage, she noticed two fellows knocking at her door.

Even in a crisis, Rahab mused, *men come, and men go.*

Sometimes they spent the night. Sometimes only a quarter of an hour. That suited her best. She needed money — real money — to prepare herself and her family for the siege.

When it came to men, her occupation made her a quick study and these two were nervous and furtive.

Still on the roof, she smiled invitingly down at them. "What is your pleasure?"

"A place for the night." The man's voice was accented like someone from the south.

A prickle of suspicion arose. Could they be the spies?

"I'll be down in a moment," she said.

She fumbled with the fabric she used to cover the flax, affording her time to weigh the possibilities. *Israelites? I think so. Perhaps I can learn something that will help Jericho fight them. Or maybe they will help me get my family out of Jericho.*

She reached the door and lifted the latch. "Come in."

One asked politely, "A place to sleep?"

"Of course."

"And a meal?"

Rahab was confused. Only a meal and a place to sleep? Nothing more?

With their thick accents, they probably asked where to find a meal and lodging, were misunderstood, and sent to me. Ah, well, money is money and I have room.

6

She watched them closely as they ate the bread she baked but would not touch the meat.

They asked many questions about Jericho. Their language and manners betrayed them. By sundown, she was certain they were spies from the Israelite camp.

"...*their God fights for them.*" She couldn't get that thought out of her head.

He might decide to rain down fire on Jericho without an Israelite picking up a sword.

Rahab was apprehensive. *Should I try to make a deal with them?*

It was only a matter of time until other men came to her door, saw the two strangers, and told Jericho's king. He would not take it kindly if she were aiding the enemy.

She had a choice: Betray the spies to the king. Or betray her friends and neighbors by helping the spies. It would have to be one or the other.

She was convinced their God would fight for them, so she made a brave and smart decision.

"You are Hebrews, are you not?"

Alarmed, the men reached for their knives. She could see the questions and fear in their eyes. Had she already betrayed them? Had she secretly sent for soldiers?

Rahab raised her hand. "Wait. I know that the Lord has given this land to you. All who live here are melting in fear because of you. We have heard how the Lord dried up the water of the Red Sea for you when you came out of Egypt, and what you did to Sihon and Og, the two kings of the Amorites east of the Jordan, whom you destroyed completely. When we heard of it, our hearts melted and everyone's courage failed because of you, for the Lord your God is God in heaven above and on the earth below."

The men listened, their expressions apprehensive, visibly weighing her words and tone for any hint of deception.

"Please swear to me by the Lord you will show kindness to my family, because I have shown kindness to you. Give me a sure sign that you will spare the lives of my father and mother, my brothers, and sisters, and all who belong to them, that you will save us from death."

The men consulted briefly with one another.

"Our lives for your lives," they assured her. "If you don't tell what we are doing, we will treat you kindly and faithfully when the Lord gives us this land."

Those were the words she wanted to hear. She would simply have to trust these men would be as good as their word.

"Then I will tell you that you are in danger here. They know there are Hebrew spies somewhere in the city and they are looking for you. The king's men may come at any moment. But I have a safe place for you to hide."

The stink of drying flax greeted them as Rahab escorted the men up the stairs to her rooftop.

"I know it smells bad, but tonight the smell is our friend. The soldiers won't come up here and they'll think you won't either."

She had no sooner rearranged the flax and cloth to cover them when heavy pounding sounded on Rahab's door.

"Shhh! You must lie very still, or you will be heard below. However, if you listen, you may hear something that will help you when you come to possess the land."

Spears and swords rattling, a cluster of soldiers stood outside the door when Rahab opened it. The soldier in charge gave her a leering wink as he proclaimed: "An order from the king of Jericho! Bring out the men who came to you and entered your house. They have come to spy out the whole land."

Rahab knew this soldier well. He was not overly burdened with brains and would be easy to mislead.

"Yes, the men came to me," she said. "But I did not know where they came from. At dusk, when it was time to close the city gate, they left."

She threw up her hands in horror at her feigned ineptitude. "I don't know which way they went. Go after them quickly! You may catch up with them."

Since money often jogged Rahab's memory, the soldier slipped a few pieces of gold into her hand and said, "If you think of anything you can tell us, you will be rewarded."

Once they left, Rahab climbed to her rooftop to watch the soldier accompanied by his men tramp off in the direction of the Jordan River. She now knew how to ensure the spies would make it back to their camp.

Rousing the spies from their hiding place, she told them, "You need to leave. Go to the hills so the pursuers will not find you. Hide yourself there three days until they return, and then go on your way.

"Please. Do not forget me."

Upon seeing a rope made of twisted red flax, one of the men pointed to it. "This oath you made us swear will not be binding when we enter the land unless you have tied this scarlet cord in the window through which you let us down and unless you have brought your father and mother, your brothers and all your family into your house. If anyone goes outside your house into the street, his blood will be on his own head; we will not be responsible. As for anyone who is in the house with you, his blood will be on our head if a hand is laid on him.

"But if you tell what we are doing, we will be released from the oath you made us swear."

"Agreed!" she replied. "Let it be as you say."

The spies slipped out the window, climbed down to the ground, and disappeared into the night.

Rahab stood at the window, listening intently to night sounds. Once she was certain the spies were safely away, she tied the scarlet rope to the frame, letting it dance in the night air.

Will You Jump Too?

"If everybody is jumping off a cliff, will you jump, too?"

This question, posed by almost every parent, is embedded throughout the Bible. God, the Heavenly Father, tells us: "If you want to be one of My followers, you must make a conscious decision to live out your faith in Me. I gave you a mind and freewill to decide.

"Or will you drift along with the crowd and jump with them to destruction?"

Let's Talk About It

I suspect Rahab's kindness was extended with mixed motives. She was highly motivated to save herself and her family. That is only right.

However, born a Canaanite, she was surrounded by the worship of multiple gods and goddesses. Some required participation in sexual rituals and the sacrifice of babies and children.

She knew what God had done to assist the Israelites already in their conquest of the land. She certainly did not want to be the enemy of the God who did that. She recognized the LORD God was truly God. Her confession of faith was this: "... for the Lord your God is God in heaven above and on the earth below." (Josh. 2:11)

Rahab realized she needed a champion to save her from destruction. She wanted to be on His side to fight for her.

Rahab never went to Sunday school, listened to a sermon, or read the Bible; nevertheless, she acknowledged His power and sovereignty. That is an important first step toward being on the right side in the war for your survival.

Warnings of Disaster Ahead

Like the warning light that comes on when your car is overheating, the people of Jericho had ample warning to confess their sin and beg for God's mercy.

You may ask, "When were they given that opportunity?"

God certainly called them to repentance. After the Israelites crossed over the Jordan, as time for the assault grew near, the people of Jericho heard what the God of Israel did, and they had time and opportunity to repent and follow Him.

In a strange, often overlooked incident, the Commander of the Army of the Lord appeared to Joshua. (Read Joshua 5:13– 15).

"Whose side are You on?" Joshua asked. (paraphrase)

"Neither. I'm here as the Commander of the Lord's Army."

"What does the Lord have to say to me?"

It turned out He had quite a lot to say to Joshua.

The Lord gave Joshua a strategy, not only for bringing down Jericho's walls, but also for simultaneously warning the citizens of Jericho of the coming destruction, calling them to repent of their bloody, immoral worship, and join with the God of Israel.

Here's how some of the invitations were issued: For six days, the Israelite army, along with seven priests carrying the Ark of the Covenant containing the Ten Commandments, marched around Jericho. On the seventh day, they marched around seven times with the Ark of the Covenant, blowing horns. But no one in the city repented or surrendered. Nor did they ask for mercy.

But Rahab did.

Is God trying to get your attention? Is there some habit, lifestyle, or relationship He wants you to leave behind? Is He — by multiple means such as marching around you, blowing trumpets, while showing something sacred — trying to get your attention so you can walk free of the walls imprisoning you?

Jesus spoke about this phenomenon: "For many are called, but few chosen." (Mt. 20:16b NIV) The whole city of Jericho was called. Only Rahab was brave enough to answer and step out from the crowd to fulfill the purpose for which she was created.

Are you?

At the End of Your Rope

Two thousand years ago, Jesus' disciples thought the end of their world was near. When they questioned Jesus about when, where, and how, He said, "You will hear of wars and rumors of wars but see to it that you are not alarmed. Such things must happen, **but the end is still to come.**" (Mt. 24:6 NIV, emphasis mine)

He encouraged His disciples not to worry so much about signs, but to be busy attending to the needs of others in Jesus' name. In the final analysis, as with Rahab, that is what will matter. (Look at Matthew 25)

Matthew quotes one of Jesus' sermons in which He urged His disciples and us to walk confidently through frightening times because God is keeping track of His own. He even knows how many hairs you have on your head. In a crisis, He's got your back. Know He will part seas and rivers ahead of you.

The Tie That Binds

Jericho, the city protected by three walls, fell. It wasn't so indestructible after all, was it? Though the walls collapsed, the lives of Rahab and her family were spared.

Sometime later, Rahab married and gave birth to Boaz. Numbered among her descendants are David, Solomon, most of the kings of Judea, and not least of all, the King of Kings, Jesus Christ of Nazareth, who said harlots and sinners would be welcomed into the kingdom of God before those who think they deserve a place in Heaven.

While the label "harlot" is almost always associated with Rahab's name, that designation is not a reproach but a testimony to the grace and mercy of God.

On the night she hid the spies, then helped them escape, she could not see into her future. She did not know what life among the Israelites would be like. Would she be a slave? A prostitute again? God who sees in secret chose to openly reward her newborn faith with mercy and a new life.

The red cord might easily have become her noose. Instead, it marked the way to escape destruction and put Rahab on the path to new life. Rahab went on to marry a Jewish man named Salmon, who founded Bethlehem. She gave birth to Boaz and raised him to be a man of high character.

Is your world under threat? Do you need a way of escape? Follow the red cord of Jesus' shed blood. He'll fight for you.

Let's Talk About Rahab

Rahab foresaw Jericho's destruction and acted when she had the opportunity. What do you see that is threatening to destroy our nation? Churches? Individuals? Families? Yourself? What steps can you take to diminish those threats?

God revealed His power and nature to Rahab prior to the spies' arrival. Where have you experienced God's presence?

Why do you think Rahab chose to make a pact with the spies rather than betray them and perhaps save Jericho?

There were likely many prostitutes in Jericho. Why do you think God chose Rahab to offer hospitality to the spies?

Do you think Rahab was a traitor to the people of Jericho? Or a realist? Or something else? Rahab made a pact with the spies to save her life and that of her family members. What steps can we take to protect our families from destructive influences both inside the home and from the outside?

Do you think God still warns people of coming judgement? Have you ever been warned by God?

The author sees the red cord as symbolic of the blood of Jesus that buys our salvation. What, if anything, do you see the red cord symbolizing?

Just between you and God:
Tell God about the situations you feel threaten your faith, family, community, etc. Ask Him what—if anything—He wants you to do to address the threat.

Chapter Two
Ruth and Naomi:
Love Makes a Dream Come True

At first glance, the book of Ruth tells a deceptively simple, almost formulaic love story. Ruth, a poor but good-hearted widow, meets a rich but lonely bachelor. They fall in love, overcome obstacles, marry, and live happily ever after.

But was it the bachelor Ruth really loved best? Or was there an unlikely rival for Ruth's heart?

What sort of love compelled Ruth to leave her family, country, and friends behind to vow commitment to another woman in words so profoundly tender they are often quoted in marriage ceremonies?

Ruth's story raises more questions. Why did she take on the responsibility of an elderly woman of no blood relation to her? Why was she willing to undertake humiliating, backbreaking labor for a fresh start at life?

Then there is the night when Ruth bathed and perfumed her body, then curled herself around the feet of an old man who was almost a stranger to her. Did she love him? Or was she simply following her mother-in-law's shrewd advice to seize an opportunity to marry well and better their situation?

In short, is the book of Ruth the story of not one gold-digger but two?

What secret did Ruth learn almost by accident that irresistibly attracted the favor of both God and man? What is the mysterious concept of "deeds are seeds"?

We will pick up valuable clues as we visit Bethlehem's barley and wheat fields and the threshing floor. We will discover what the Scriptures say about what sort of love story was really going on between Ruth and Naomi.

In this study from the Book of Ruth we will learn:
- ✓ The principle of "deeds are seeds."
- ✓ A pattern for committed love.
- ✓ How to thrive in a crisis.
- ✓ How God can repair shattered dreams.

Bringing in the Sheaves

The book of Ruth, possibly penned by the prophet Samuel in approximately 1100 BC, has Bethlehem as the background for Ruth and Naomi's story.

You might think Bethlehem was a quiet little town with glitter on the house roofs and a "No Vacancy" sign flashing above the Motel 6. But for many years before Bethlehem hosted Mary and Joseph, it was a hard-working farming community.

In Ruth and Naomi's day, harvest was an all-consuming event. Leaving a crop standing in the field invited starvation and Bethlehem had just survived that. Fear of returning hunger was a motivator, so every able-bodied person, young or old, male, or female, took part in the barley harvest.

Depending upon the level of ripeness of the grain, workers either pulled the entire barley plant out of the ground or scythed off the stalks. When gathered, wrapped into bouquet-like bunches, and stacked into larger bundles, they were known as sheaves.

Over-ripe heads of barley shattered when touched. The Law of Moses instructed these kernels be left where they fell for the poor or wayfarer to pick up. This is a backbreaking one-kernel-at-a-time harvesting known as gleaning. (Read Leviticus 23:22)

Keep this information in mind as you walk in the sandals of Ruth and Naomi.

Winds of Change
Naomi's Story — Part 1

Three women, one old and two young, stood at the ford of the Jordan River. Behind them towered the Moab mountains. Ahead was the unknowable. Crossing the river might make Naomi's long-cherished dream come true. Or lead to more disappointment. Whatever the outcome, at the end of their journey, she would be in Bethlehem, the hometown she wished she'd never left.

What would drive someone to leave the land and everyone she knew to slave in the fields of her country's enemy? For Naomi, it was seeing the starvation-pinched faces of her growing boys. Her own gnawing hunger. Family and neighbors dying of starvation. Drinking muddy water from the drying village well and being grateful for it. Sun-bleached fields producing nothing but dust — constant, windblown, powder-fine, and choking.

Naomi remembered the day her husband whispered, "We've eaten all the seed we saved for next year's crop. If God sent rain now, we would have nothing to plant. Let's take the boys and cross the river to work as hired hands in the fields of Moab."

Hoping to leave trouble behind, they entered Moab, a land with strange customs and languages and idol worship. Rather than a change of fortune, they simply traded one disaster for another. Looking back, Naomi wasn't sure how she survived the last ten years.

First, her husband died.

Her sons came of age and married. This, too, was a disappointment. Like any Jewish mother, she wanted her boys to marry women who shared their customs and religion. But no. They married Moabite women. First came daughter-in-law Orpah. Then Ruth.

But no grandchildren. No babies or childish laughter to brighten their tents and carry on the family name.

Then came the final tragedy. Both Naomi's sons died, leaving three women without male protection, so necessary in their culture.

What was left to live for? Naomi couldn't think of a thing.

According to local custom, it fell to the dead husband's family to provide a dowry and mate for a widowed daughter-in-law. This was simply impossible. Naomi could barely feed herself.

God, please don't abandon me too, she prayed often.

From afar came a spark of hope. After years of drought, rain finally returned to Judah. The barley harvest in Bethlehem looked promising. At last, God was sending bread.

Naomi perked up. "I own land in Bethlehem," she explained to Ruth and Orpah. "I can again live among my own people. All that holds me in Moab are three graves. And you. So go back to your mothers' houses. May God grant you rest in the home of another husband."

Over the last years, the three women often wept together. This would be the last time.

Naomi straightened her shoulders, and nearly running, headed west toward the Jordan River.

Unbeknown to Naomi, someone was watching. And following.

Ruth's Story — Part 1

Returning to her mother did not appeal to Ruth. No caring or affection existed there. But in Naomi's ragged tent, she felt genuinely loved. And she wanted to go with Naomi. But would Naomi's people accept her? Jews looked with suspicious contempt on Moabites. They might drive her away. Or kill her.

Ruth looked west across the Jordan River. On the far shore was the unknown. But if Naomi's people were anything like her, Ruth wanted to live among them. Through her mother-in-law, Ruth had learned about the God of the Israelites. Vastly different than the Moabite gods, He was not made of wood or stone. He didn't live on a shelf in a shrine. He was everywhere. And wonder of wonders, He knew her name.

Home was where Naomi was. Ruth decided it was time to declare it.

"Don't urge me to turn my back on you," Ruth said to her mother-in-law. "Where you go, I will go. Where you stay, I will stay. Your people will be my people: your God, my God. Where you die, I will die, and there I will be buried. May the LORD deal with me severely if anything but death separates you and me." (Read Ruth 1:16-18)

Naomi's Story — Part 2

As they neared Bethlehem, harvesters stopped, scythes poised in midair, to stare at the two women traveling alone through the ripening fields of Judah.

"Who are they? Where are their men? The old one — she looks familiar. She's a Jew. The young one — foreign. A Moabite? Perhaps a slave? Or a spy? A fugitive?"

Grief and time had not been kind to Naomi's face; but within minutes of her arrival, Bethlehem recognized the older woman.

"Naomi!" the women cried. "Is it really you?"

"I used to be Naomi (pleasant)," she told them. "Don't call me that anymore. Call me Mara (bitterness) because I went away full of life and have returned drained. The LORD has brought misfortune upon me."

The women nodded. They had losses too.

Ruth's story — Part 2

Ruth watched as friends and relatives of Naomi's warmly welcomed her. Toward Ruth, the townsfolk remained guarded. Moabites had a bad reputation. Attitudes softened some when Naomi explained who Ruth was and why she was there.

Despite the shortage of harvesters, none offered Ruth work in their fields. She needed a way to feed them until they could grow their own crops.

"Let me glean in the fields wherever anyone will let me," Ruth suggested to Naomi.

A tedious, degrading job, it took keen eyesight and a young back. It could also be dangerous. Unprotected and alone, Ruth might be attacked in the fields. If only there were another way to earn their bread.

At first light, Ruth approached the foreman. "May I glean?"

Harvesters, sharpening their scythes, stared at Ruth.

The foreman had heard of Ruth. He nodded curtly and pointed at the tent pitched at the edge of the field. "When you need to rest, use the shelter with the other girls."

Face to the ground and nearly on her knees, Ruth parted scratchy undergrowth searching for grain. A pale speck of barley winked at her. She picked out the granule and deposited it in her pouch. One grain. An hour passed before she had a small handful. By the time she took a short rest from the sun's glare, she had a generous handful, perhaps enough for a meal for Naomi.

"Boaz is coming!" Gossip and jesting stopped. Everyone worked conscientiously as an older man arrived.

"The LORD be with you!" Boaz called out to the workers.

The workers bowed. Their response was warm and heartfelt: "The LORD bless you!"

The workers returned to harvesting as Boaz appraised their progress. As Ruth painfully straightened her back, she caught his eye.

She noted Boaz and his foreman discussing her. She put her head down, frantically searching for more grain as she heard their footfalls coming toward her. Would she be told to leave? Would they confiscate what she had gleaned? Or would they want another form of payment? Anything was possible.

The two men stood before her. Boaz spoke: "My daughter."

Ruth glanced at him, confused by his kindly greeting. Boaz had a strong face and vigorous frame, yet he was older than she first thought.

"Don't glean in other fields. Stay near my servant girls. You'll be safe here. I've given the men orders that you are not to be bothered." He pointed to the water skins hanging inside the tents. "When you are thirsty, drink from the water my men have drawn."

Ruth stared at his feet. "Why are you so kind to me—a foreigner?"

Boaz said, "I've heard what you have done for your mother-in-law since the death of your husband. How you left your own father and mother and homeland to live with strangers. The LORD will repay you. May you be richly rewarded by the God of Israel under whose wings you take refuge."

"God's wings of refuge." The man has the heart of a poet, thought Ruth. (Ps. 17:8, 36:7, 57:1, 61:4, 63:7, 91:4)

"I hope you continue to think well of me, my lord," she said. "Your kind words comfort me although I am not even one of your servants."

Soon the inviting aroma of toasting barley wafted over the field. Her stomach rumbled as Ruth continued to glean while the rest stopped to eat.

"Ruth! Come here!" Boaz called to her from the tent. He pointed to piles of fresh bread and a bowl of wine vinegar, olive oil, and salty spices.

"Have some bread. Dip it in the wine vinegar."

He tore off a hunk, dipped it, and popped it in his mouth. "It's good. Try it."

She found the soaked bread surprisingly refreshing as she sat with the female harvesters to eat.

Boaz appeared at her elbow. "Toasted barley?" he asked.

She nodded. He poured a generous scoopful into her lap. Rubbing the still warm grain between her hands until the chaff flew away, she ate the kernels.

What is Naomi eating? Tonight, we feast on barley!

As she returned to the field, she heard Boaz speak her name. She turned to look. He was addressing the male harvesters before they went out to pick up the stacked sheaves. She couldn't hear what he said to them. Then, inexplicably, she found a bundle of barley stalks lying in her path. She was horrified at the carelessness of the harvesters until she noticed the harvesters making little bouquets of barley when they picked up the sheaves and laying them in her path. They furtively watched Ruth to see what she would do.

Boaz was watching, too.

Then she knew. Ruth's kindness to Naomi prompted kindness from Boaz. (C)

Some men are bold romantics, presenting garlands of roses to their sweethearts.

Other men are practical. The practical man replaces blown car fuses, changes hard-to-reach light bulbs, makes dinner when his love is working late, empties mousetraps — all subtle bouquets from a man whose concern is his lady's wellbeing.

Little nosegays of ripe barley scattered over a field — a shy but practical bachelor farmer's bouquets of appreciation to a hardworking girl. What could be more appropriate?

Or was it meant to ask Naomi a question?

Naomi's story — Part 3

Ruth opened the top of her bag so her mother-in-law could admire the contents.

"So much barley!" Naomi murmured. "Another gift from Boaz?"

Ruth nodded.

"Anything happen?" Naomi asked.

"No."

From the first day she spent in Boaz's fields, Ruth — and all the fieldhands — were aware she had caught his admiring eye. Daily, he ensured Ruth returned to Naomi with a load of barley. After six weeks, the barley harvest was coming to an end. The next harvest was wheat. Yet after nearly daily contact and gifts of grain, he had not made a single move to make her his wife. What was holding him back?

"Hmm..." The old woman thought aloud, "He's cautious. He wants to care for you, but he fears becoming a lovesick old fool chasing a much younger woman. He needs to know you would be willing to marry him."

Naomi stood in the doorway, looking at the level windswept plateau at the edge of the village fields that was the threshing floor. A small cooking fire was kindled there and clouds of chaff from winnowing blew into the twilight.

"Boaz is our near kinsman," Naomi mused aloud. "And I need to find a home and husband for you. Look."

Ruth's eyes followed Naomi's finger to Boaz silhouetted against the sunset.

"He is winnowing barley tonight. Wash and perfume yourself. Put on your best clothes and go there but stay hidden until he has finished eating and drinking. Notice where he lies down. Uncover his feet and lie down. He will tell you what to do."

Ruth's story — Part 3

Ruth considered her mother-in-law's words. To throw herself at his feet, to present herself to him and ask for his protection was a bold plan. And risky. They might have misread his generosity and she would be humiliated.

"I will do all you say to me," Ruth told her mother-in-law.

Later, Ruth stealthily stepped onto the threshing floor and sat in the dark shadows.

After years of drought and long days of hard fieldwork, everyone was celebrating a bountiful harvest. To the jingle of tambourines and the rhythm of clapping hands, they danced with jubilant abandon, singing ancient songs praising God.

"Your people pass into Canaan, O Lord; "The people whom You have purchased.

"You bring them into the land and plant them on Your own mountain, O Lord.

"You will reign forever and ever!"

(Ex. 15: 16a-19)

Wine flowed and laughter was genuine.

As the fire died to low embers, haunting melodies from a shepherd's lyre and flute echoed through the night. One by one, the men rolled their cloaks around themselves and slept.

Ruth watched from the deep shadows, barely daring to breathe. Soon all the harvesters slept, but Boaz and another man. They sat near the fire, talking in low tones, occasionally laughing. Finally, she heard Boaz wish the man, "Shalom."

After checking the threshing floor's perimeter, Boaz lay down at the end of the heaps to guard the grain. Instantly, his breathing became deep and regular.

With pounding heart, Ruth approached. Stealthily, she uncovered Boaz's feet. He sighed in his sleep but did not move. She curled her body around his feet and covered them with her robe. And waited.

"Thieves! Raiders to steal the harvest!"

Boaz sprang upright, then realized it was only a dream. He rubbed his eyes. As he turned over, he felt the soft warmth at his feet. When he looked, he discovered a woman lying there.

"Who are you? What do you want?"

"I am Ruth, your maidservant."

Then she quoted back to him his poetic blessing from their first meeting: "Spread your wing of protection over me. You are my next of kin. You have the right to marry me."

"God bless you. You are kinder to me than you are to Naomi. You have not sought young men, either poor or rich. Now don't worry. I will do for you all you require. Everyone knows you are a woman of worth and courage.

"There is, however, a kinsman nearer to you than I am. If he will perform for you the part of a kinsman redeemer, let him do it. But if he will not or cannot, then, as the Lord lives, I will. Lie down until the morning."

Ruth and Boaz talked in low tones until early morning. She told him of her life in Moab and why she followed Naomi to Bethlehem. He told her things about himself that he had never told anyone.

Dawn was drawing near.

"You need to go home. But I don't want to send you back to your mother-in-law empty-handed. Bring your mantle."

He scooped six measures of barley into it, tied it into a bundle, and helped her put it on. He led her past sleeping men to the path back to Bethlehem.

"Let's keep it our secret that you were here."

With false dawn lighting the way, she walked back to town with hopeful news for her mother-in-law.

But with hope came new fear. Boaz's words repeated in her head: "There is, however, a kinsman nearer to you than I am."

Before sunset, a stranger might claim her for his wife.

A Dynasty Begins

"Boaz will not rest until the matter is settled," Naomi told Ruth. "And he'll settle it today. You'll soon know."

Naomi was a shrewd judge of character. And correct. Boaz was a get-it-done sort of guy.

Immediately, he went to the gates of Bethlehem where all public business was transacted before witnesses. Contracts required three witnesses. Boaz wanted ten. A careful businessman, he was determined there be no ambiguity. He had a strategy.

"Brother!" Boaz called to the kinsman as he entered the city. "Come.

I have a once-in-a-lifetime opportunity for you.

"Did you know our relative Naomi has returned from Moab? Her husband and both sons are dead. She is in desperate need of money. Fortunately, she has land to sell. Do you want to buy it? If not, I will. But you have first right of refusal. Of course, the land needs to stay in our family."

"Yes! I do want to buy it." The kinsman was excited at the prospect.

Boaz said, "To buy the land you must marry the widow, Ruth of Moab, since she also has ownership of the land."

The kinsman knew his happy home would instantly become an unhappy one if he brought home a second wife. What was more, he would endanger his inheritance. Maybe his life too.

Reluctantly, he said. "I can't. You buy the property and marry the widow."

In the customary fashion for transferring property, the kinsman handed Boaz his sandal.

Holding the kinsman's sandal aloft so everyone could see, Boaz announced his intentions.

"Today, you are all witnesses. I have bought from Naomi all the property of Elimelech, Kilion and Mahlon and I will acquire Ruth as my wife."

Ruth became the wife of Boaz.

The relationship between Ruth and Naomi continued and deepened when Ruth gave birth to a son. They named him Obed, which means "servant or worker." Naomi cared for little Obed. He was considered her grandson, the continuation of her life, and a memorial to her lost husband and sons.

"Naomi has a son!" the women of Bethlehem said. "Praise be to the LORD. He has not left you without a kinsman-redeemer. And your daughter-in-law is kinder to you than seven sons.

"May this child become famous throughout Israel! He will renew your life and sustain you in your old age."

The End of Their Story, the Beginning of Yours

What drew Boaz immediately to Ruth?

Their instant attraction for one another is not so unusual when you consider Boaz's mother, Rahab. (Josh. 6; Mt. 1:5)

Today, Rahab is a heroine to Jews. But in Boaz's day, she was a Canaanite and former prostitute—true deterrents to matrimony. Despite Boaz's good character and wealth, his mixed heritage may have been a problem for some Bethlehem families of his day, contributing to his bachelor status.

Plucky and enterprising, Rahab chose to leave her own people and join the children of God. She risked herself to save her family.

This can also be said of Ruth.

For Boaz, it wasn't about indefinable notions of romantic love, a pretty face, or how well Ruth filled out her tunic. Boaz saw substantive qualities in Ruth, such as kindness, industriousness, accountability, courage, faith, and more. His masculine essence responded. He wanted to protect and serve her.

Naomi's Secret

Naomi had a secret: She was not merely Ruth's mother-in-law. Most importantly, she was her spiritual mother. Surprisingly, she may be yours, too.

While living in Naomi's tent and sharing her mother-in-law's life, Ruth saw Naomi fight back against the bad, ugly, and heartbreaking. Ruth thought, *If the Jews' God is faithful in tragedy, He can be counted on in the day-to-day rough-and-tumble of life.*

Ruth was attracted to Naomi's faith because God gave Naomi courage and wisdom to creatively face the hard knocks of life. Seeing Naomi's faith in God during multiple tragedies was inspiring enough to cause Ruth to abandon her former life, natural parents, country, and gods.

Naomi's faith gave birth to Ruth's faith, and Naomi became her spiritual mother.

Your Story:

Are you a Ruth? Are your dreams on hold while you care for another? There is a God who rewards selflessness.

Are you a Naomi? Are you disappointed with life, assuming all your hopes are dashed, all your dreams dead? There is a good God on the throne, and He wants to help you reach your goals.

Trust your dreams to the Lord. He specializes in bringing life to barren ground.

Just as Ruth watched Naomi struggle through one heartbreak after another, someone has been watching you, too. She may be in your home, church, neighborhood, or place of business. You may not know her name, but she knows you. She is watching to see how you handle the bumps of life.

Freaked out? Don't think your life is perfect enough to introduce others to God? Seekers understand that it would be easy to follow God if He paid the faithful by making a believer happy and prosperous. That doesn't resonate with real life.

Sometimes, seekers—and believers—need to see how a Christ-follower deals with a sick child, bad health, or financial setbacks. In difficult circumstances, seekers can see God at work gifting His children with serenity, joy, peace, and strength. And they want to know Him. They want Him involved in their day-to-day joys and sorrows.

In most cultures, no one gets any less respect than mothers-in-law and postmenopausal women. In the late autumn of Naomi's life, at a moment when women were considered dried up, used up, and worthless, because of her gift of faith in God, she inspired one of the world's most amazing declarations of committed love. (F)

Naomi's secret? As described in Titus 2, a down-on-her-luck lone woman shared her life and faith in God with those closest to her. Her faith began a dynasty of faith: Obed was the father of Jesse; Jesse was the father of King David: David was the ancestor of Jesus.

At work were two bedrock principles written by God across the cosmos:

1. If what you do for others is based on what you can get out of it, you will not prosper but reap a crop of weeds. God tells us to think beyond our immediate needs to loving our neighbor — or mother-in-law — as ourselves.
2. Sow deeds that please His Spirit. From His Spirit you will receive life at the proper season. Don't give up! Only the Spirit of God knows when the harvest will come and what sort of juicy, ripe, eternal fruit will fall from God's hands into yours.

If you are a follower of Jesus, Ruth and Naomi's faith lives in you, too. Their deeds were seeds of faith. Isn't it surprising where they sprouted?

Let's Talk About Ruth and Naomi

A. Who was your spiritual mentor? Tell us what she/he did to help you grow spiritually.
B. Have you ever acted as a spiritual mentor to another? Tell us about your experience. Was it rewarding? Disappointing? Difficult?
C. Some call it Karma. The Bible says, "You reap what you sow" twenty-eight times with slightly different wording but they nearly all mean the same thing. Some examples are Galatians 6:7 , 2 Corinthians 9:6, and Psalm 126:5, all wording from the NIV. Have you ever seen or experienced evidence of the "deeds are seeds" concept?
D. Read Ruth's pledge to Naomi in Ruth 1:16-17. Can you describe the sort of person who would inspire this type of loyalty?
E. We often hear about parents adopting children, but rarely of children adopting parents as Ruth did Naomi. What reasons do you think someone would have for turning their back on their life, family, country, and gods to adopt another way of life?
F. What types of relationships foster a closer walk with God? What

types of relationships cause people to wander away from Him?

Just Between You and God
Read 2 Corinthians 12: 7b-10.
Ask God: Are there any relationships You want to me to give up to grow closer to You?

Chapter Three
Deborah the Prophetess:
How Her Strategy Won a War

Let's Talk About Deborah

No doubt about it: Deborah the prophetess makes people nervous. (Judges 4 and 5)

Why? Perhaps because she doesn't fit the stereotypical demure-little-woman mold. Or perhaps because Deborah was courageous, and her courage strikes terror and conviction in the fainthearted. Maybe because her God-given prophetic vision saw people as they truly were.

Or perhaps Deborah — whose name means "bee" — personified her fierce but valuable little namesake with sweetness for her people and a sting for their enemies.

Or maybe it was because she goaded the terrified into facing the object of their fear. (A)

That's what Deborah did. She inspired a visionless leader and his nervous army to face impossible odds in the name of the Lord.

Whatever the reason, she packed a punch in her day. She still does.

We know only snippets of Deborah's private life. For example, her husband's name was Lappidoth (means "a light") and she felt called to be a mother to Israel. (Read Judges 5:7) Jews all over the world consider her a mother to their race, nation, and religion.

Why does this motherly woman cause nervousness after thousands of years? Is it because she knew how to motivate people to do the right thing despite their fears?

We'll find out as we look at Deborah the prophetess and the battle she helped win.

The Winding River

On one of my visits to Israel ...

From the summit of Mount Tabor, a blazing sunset stretches over the Jezreel Valley. Below, the River Kishon (its name means "winding") winks reflected light as it twists through the valley.

Most of the year, the Kishon seems tame. Don't be fooled. Let a cloudburst take place in the faraway western mountains and meek little

Kishon becomes a raging torrent. Remember this. It's an important clue to Deborah's victory.

In the twilight, Gabrielle, a former captain of the Israeli army, surveys the valley for defensive and offensive positions.

Gabrielle says, "The Jezreel Valley (also known as the Valley of Armageddon) is a perfect battleground. King Saul and his sons and King Josiah all died in battles here. Gideon fought and defeated the Midianites here. The final battle in Revelation will be fought here. And of course, Deborah and Barak fought here."

Gabrielle's finger points out the convoluted ribbon of the Kishon.

"The earth is porous around the Kishon. It soaks up and holds moisture. Long ago, when the river flooded, it became a quagmire. Today, we have better, more sophisticated ways of managing water.

"While most Israeli women serve in the army," she says, "they do not serve in combat positions. The sheer physical strain of battle is considered too much for women. In shoulder-to-shoulder fighting with male soldiers, it is thought that men would take risks to protect the women."

How would men fight if they had only one woman to protect? And what if they saw that lone woman as their mother?

A Date Under the Palm (B)
Between Ramah and Bethel
Between 1209 BC and 1169 BC

Wind rippled the palm fronds above Deborah and blew up skiffs of dust.

A change in the weather is coming, thought Deborah. *The dry season will soon end.*

Today Deborah would decide legal matters for the people of the land. Families with disputes, neighbors with property questions, parents with unruly children, accused thieves, widows cheated out of their inheritance — the line of people waiting for her words of wisdom snaked behind the palm where she sat, and circled around.

Oh Lord, I need Your wisdom and words.

A Galilean farmer stepped forward to present his case.

"Mother Deborah, many times our village has been pillaged by King Jabin's army. They steal our crops. They take our sons and daughters as slaves. On the high places they worship Baal. Is there no God in Israel?"

"What is your tribe?"

"Naphtali."

Because of their proximity to King Jabin's capital city of Hazor, she knew the tribes formed by the descendants of Naphtali and Zebulun suffered from harassment from Sisera, commander of the Canaanite armies.

But they were under God's judgement. Had they suffered enough to willingly take up arms and expel the Canaanites as God instructed a long time ago? Had they repented? Had they turned to God?

"Do the people of your village still sacrifice to Baal?"

"We did, Mother Deborah. But we have cut down the sacred groves and smashed the idols."

"Repentance is more than smashing idols and saying, 'I'm sorry.' It is actively following God. If God said, 'Take up arms against Sisera,' would your village do this? Would you?"

Before straightening his shoulders and looking Deborah in the eye, the farmer said, "Sisera has 900 iron chariots. His men have swords. We have only farm tools and walking staffs. (Read Judges 5:8) But if the God of Israel says to me, 'Fight Sisera,' I will fight him. I cannot speak for my village.

"Mother, shall I leave my farm and join with Barak? He is attempting to raise an army."

Deborah had waited twenty years to hear these words.

"I have a task for you. Go to Barak. Tell him Deborah has a word from the Lord for him and he is to come to me to receive it."

The farmer's face lit with hope. "I'll do it, Mother! Whatever you say."

She watched the farmer trudge toward Galilee.

That's one soldier. What will it take before the rest of the men of Galilee are willing to fight?

Mother Said So

Nose to nose, Deborah and Barak faced off.

"Didn't the LORD God of Israel command you, 'Deploy troops at Mount Tabor on the River Kishon'?"

Barak squirmed and ran his finger around the neck of his robe.

She pressed him. "Didn't God say to you, 'Take ten thousand men of Naphtali and Zebulun against Sisera, the commander of Jabin's army and I will deliver him into your hand'?"

Barak had indeed heard the voice of God, but many would-be soldiers didn't believe Barak — or God — was realistic about their chances of defeating Sisera and Jabin. They had a formidable, well-trained, well-equipped army. Their 900 iron chariots were pulled by powerful horses. They had bronze weaponry. The men of Israel had only their farm implements.

On top of that, Barak was wishy-washy. One day, he was confident they could defeat Sisera. The next day, he wasn't sure.

The time was ripe. It was God's season of deliverance. Deborah knew it would be better for Israel if Barak would follow God out of obedience and trust. But he still held back, vacillating between fear and faith in God. Someone needed to deliver the people.

Finally, Barak spoke. "If you go with me, I will go. But if you won't, I will not go." (Read Judges 4:6–8. Here it is paraphrased.)

If Barak was afraid to follow God into battle, she was not.

"All right. I will go with you. But because of the way you are going about this, the honor will not be yours. The LORD will hand Sisera over to a woman." (Read Judges 4:9–paraphrase) (C)

Women Who Go to Battle

Want an interesting study? Look at the life of Joan of Arc. Or Boadicea. Or Golda Meir. These women compare with Deborah as military leaders who battled invaders to protect their children, homes, families, and nations. Special endowments and circumstances combine to mold women or men into military leaders. Women have often gone to war but rarely as military leaders.

Disguised as men, some women have fought alongside husbands, sons, or lovers. More typically, women supported soldiers by providing medical or sanitary aid and comfort.

But what does it take to make a woman into a prophetess? Criterion for a prophetess or prophet is very stringent. One false word and he or she is to be put to death.

To be a prophetess requires a woman, especially called by God, to willingly sacrifice herself to stand between God and those in opposition to Him. She must be courageous enough to speak absolute truth on behalf of God.

She must accept personal attacks when delivering God's message. She may become a target by refusing to deliver false but politically correct messages.

More than military leaders or prophetesses, the world needs women who will follow the steps of Deborah. Warrior women who protect themselves against Satan. They must accept personal attacks when delivering God's message. Women who battle against destroyers of marriages, children, nations, and churches. Women who recognize the army of God only marches forward on its knees. (Read Ephesians 6:10–18)

What great good would happen in our world if godly women from every nation went to battle against evil? What great good could happen in your community if the women warriors in your church devoted themselves to strapping on the armor of God and by using defensive weapons defeat Satan? What would happen in your home if you did?

"The Lord Will Fight for Us"

Atop Mount Tabor, Barak and Deborah saw Sisera's 900 iron chariots approach. They journeyed up the Jezreel Valley to the foot of Mt. Tabor. At the front of the advancing column rode Sisera.

Barak's ragtag army, largely comprised of farmers and shepherds, paused in their efforts to dig trenches in Tabor's limestone slopes to watch maneuvers below them. With military precision, the Canaanite army formed a wall around the base of the mountain. Between chariots, armored foot soldiers moved into position. It was an impressive display. And fear inspiring.

"We're dead men," one man said.

His companion nudged him. "Have you less courage than a woman? Israel's mother is with us. She'll tell us what the Lord says. You'll see. The Lord will fight for us."

A scout reported to Barak. "Since their horses need water, Sisera's army is making camp along the Kishon River. But there is rain upon the western mountains."

Deborah turned to Barak. "Quick! The LORD has gone ahead of you! Muster the soldiers to attack for this is the moment the LORD has given Sisera into your hands."

At Barak's signal, the ram's horn echoed on the mountain.

Barak shouted, "Charge!".

His army picked up their pitchforks, hoes, and courage to run down Mount Tabor to engage the enemy.

From the summit, Deborah saw what the Israelite army could not. The Kishon River was swelling. The earth shuddered. Within minutes, a flash flood roared up the river valley.

In the wake of the torrent, the porous earth melted into a sea of mire, pulling under iron chariots and heavily armored soldiers. Chariot horses thrashed frantically, trying to escape the suffocating mud.

After years of oppression, the Israelite army took revenge on their enemy. Not a Canaanite was left alive.

The land had peace for forty years.

Guess what happened to Sisera? (Read Judges 4:17-22)

Where's Deborah on Mother's Day?

Remember the story of the Little Red Hen? When no one would help her, she did it all herself.

Deborah is like the Little Red Hen. When everyone who should have taken the lead chickened out, she stepped up for the glory of God and the good of her nation.

Although Deborah calls herself "a mother to Israel," the prophetess's story is seldom told on Mother's Day, probably because she still makes some feel ashamed for their fears and inaction. But when some of the men of Israel found courage to fight back against marauding Canaanites, the nation had forty years of peace.

And Sisera? What happened to him? Read the rest of Judges 4. You'll see he got "the point."

Frustrated and frightened by the evil that is entrenched in your world? Do you see needs that should be met, rights needing to be championed, wrongs needing to be addressed? Do you want to see truth, justice, and righteousness prevail?

Maybe *you* are called to follow in the footsteps of Deborah the prophetess to wage war against evil. (D)

Let's Talk About Deborah
A. How do you feel about women leaders? Why do you think strong women like Deborah sometimes make some nervous?
B. What kind of person does it take to arbitrate legal matters and give sage personal advice? To whom do you look for sound advice?
C. Why do you think Barak was afraid to go to battle without Deborah?
D. Imagine you are a modern-day Deborah. What great evil in the world would you fight? What would you do? What can you do?
E. What qualities of Deborah would you like to emulate?

Just Between You and God
God, You called me to stand against evil in the world. What should I do and how shall I do it?

Chapter Four
Bathsheba:
Temptress or Victim?

War, conspiracy, murder — all these elements comprise the epic "love story" of Bathsheba and David.

We may think we know how Bathsheba became the undoing of a king. However, when we take a closer look and learn more about Iron Age culture and religious observances, you may be surprised at what we discover.

Renaissance paintings often depict Bathsheba as a voluptuous beauty lingering in a bubble bath, coyly exposing her charms to tempt a saintly King David. You may be in for some stunning surprises as we separate fact from fiction.

You may discover Bathsheba is a woman you want to emulate.

Although she is known as a seductress, she is far more than that. We will meet the real Bathsheba and learn her secret for not just surviving a bad situation but transforming it.

Through Bathsheba's story we will answer these three questions:
✓ Can a marriage that starts out wrong ever be right?
✓ Can a victim overcome the wrong done to her and develop a healthy relationship with her abuser?
✓ Do you owe Bathsheba an apology for your impression of her?

City of David: The Scene of the Crimes

We only need to stand on the crest of the Silwan Valley, the site of the ancient City of David where the drama in Bathsheba's story played out, to see what King David might have seen.

And what he did not see.

At the foot of the valley is the site of the ancient City of David. It lies cheek-to-jowl with the Old City on one of the jutting hipbones of Mount Zion. While the gorge is densely populated, excavations are turning up some amazing archeological discoveries of Israel's most famous warrior

31

and king. From the zenith, King David ruled from his palace.

Men in High Places
Read 2 Samuel 5: 9-11

From David's elevated terraces, invading armies could be spotted approaching from any direction. Here David saw something that threatened his kingship more than invaders: a bathing Bathsheba.

While the panorama view of Jerusalem is spectacular from ground level, it must have been truly impressive when David's palace stood there. From the flat rooftop, David could see beyond the city walls and any enemy's approach.

Remember this. David's rooftop view is an important clue to the real story of Bathsheba.

One life-changing night, David had insomnia. Perhaps his mind was at work composing yet another of his 300+ poems and psalms. Whatever he was thinking became insignificant because his actions personified Proverbs 16:27a: *Idle hands are the devil's workshop.*

We'll see what David saw. It may surprise you to discover what he didn't see.

Meet Bathsheba. What does the Bible tell us about her?

✓ Bathsheba was a favorite with her father. Unlike many fathers who only valued sons, her father, Eliam, was so delighted at her birth that he named her Bathshua (1 Chron. 3:5), meaning "daughter of my prosperity or "I'm rich! I have a daughter!" As her personality developed, her name was changed to Bathsheba.

✓ The *Hebrew to English Dictionary* says: "Seventh daughter" is the literal translation, but it also could be interpreted "the perfect woman" or "daughter of an oath."

✓ The men in Bathsheba's family were highly placed in King David's administration. Not only was Bathsheba's father, Eliam (also known as Ammiel, 2 Sam. 11:3 and 1 Chron. 3:5) one of David's thirty-seven most trusted men (2 Sam. 23:34), but her husband, Uriah, was highly placed too.

✓ Bathsheba's grandfather Ahithophel was David's trusted advisor. (2 Sam. 16:23, 2 Sam. 23:34) He advised David on maintaining peace between warring tribes. His word was said to be like "the voice of God" in David's ear.

✓ Bathsheba was a very pretty woman. (2 Sam. 11:2b) Then as now, people talk. David may have heard rumors of Bathsheba's great beauty.

✓ Bathsheba was married to Uriah the Hittite. Apparently, she loved her warrior husband. We know that because of her reaction to his death. (2 Sam. 11:26)

Meet Uriah. What does the Bible tell us about him?

✓ Along with his wife's father, he fought alongside David. David trusted Uriah with his life. (1 Chron. 11:41)

✓ Uriah was one of David's thirty-seven most trusted men. (2 Sam. 23:34)

✓ It takes a special woman to be married to a man who daily puts his very life on the line. Bathsheba was one of those women. Her father was a warrior so when she married Uriah — also a warrior — she knew she was signing up for possible widowhood. She must have thought Uriah worth the risk because he proved to be a man everyone could rely on until the bitter end.

✓ Uriah was disciplined. (2 Sam. 11:9-13) Soldiers were to be celibate. (1 Sam. 21:4, 5)

✓ Uriah, whose name means "Yahweh is my light" was probably a convert to Judaism or a Jew who lived in the Hittite area. (2 Sam. 11:11)

✓ Uriah was very fond of his wife. The description of his loving attachment to her is heartbreaking when you consider their violent parting. (2 Sam. 12:3) **(B)**

A Fling with a King? Or No Escape from a Rape?

When a woman has her regular flow of blood, the impurity of her monthly period will last seven days... she must count off seven days, and after that she will be ceremonially clean. (Lev. 15:19, 28b)

Perhaps Bathsheba chose a spray of orange pomegranate blossoms as the first sight greeting Uriah when — and if — he came through their door. Something like that may have been a subtle signal between Uriah and Bathsheba that she was ceremonially clean and they could enjoy relations. We must admit a secret message delivered like that inviting him to visit her bed is much more romantic than Uriah declaring, "Hubba! Hubba, Bathsheba!"

According to Jewish Law, sexual intimacy between husband and wife was forbidden for nearly half of each month. Those days were determined by her period.

A clue: At the conclusion of those days, when the sun has set and the first stars appear, a wife would visit the mikveh.

A mikveh is very much like an outdoor baptismal tank with steps leading down into the water. For both men and women, ritual bathing in the mikveh was central to Jewish family life and religious worship.

After her visit to the mikveh, a woman could discreetly invite her husband to her bed with their secret signal.

In Bathsheba's day, worship was not haphazard or spontaneous. To approach God, a woman (or a man) performed ritual cleansing of the body to prepare for cleansing the soul. The mikveh was key to this.

Old Testament laws governing family purity, known as *Taharat Hamishpacha*, are based on two concepts: *taharah* (spiritually pure) and *tumah* (spiritually impure). These two opposing values relate spiritual cleanliness to physical cleanliness and spiritual impurity to physical impurity. (For more information, use the search terms *Taharat Hamishpacha*.)

What Sort of Bath?

She had purified herself from her uncleanness... (2 Sam. 11:4)

Before visiting the mikveh, Bathsheba prepared by first taking a hygienic bath, untangling her hair, and cleaning her teeth.

Some artists have painted David observing Bathsheba taking her pre-mikveh wash. Others depict Bathsheba lingering in a posh bathtub, although a bath in ancient days was anything but a sensual delight.

Keep in mind every drop of water in the City of David or Jerusalem either had to be hauled uphill from the Gihon Spring in the valley below David's palace or came from rainwater collected in cisterns. Moreover, nudity was objectionable and privacy scarce, so hygienic bathing required some maneuvering.

A Bedouin woman, whose way of life preserves ancient skills, showed me how women executed a hygienic bath long ago in cramped quarters. After warming a small pot of water in the sunshine, she loosened her waistband, straddled the pot, and dropped her dress over it. Pulling her arms inside her sleeves without removing her dress, she scrubbed herself beneath her clothing.

Do you think David was enflamed with desire as he observed Bathsheba in the twilight wiggling inside her clothes? Stranger things have happened. However, if that were the case, David imagined much more than he saw because this sort of bath could be executed in bright sunshine on a busy street without exposing an inch of skin.

As she prepared to visit the mikveh, we may wonder if Bathsheba assumed her bed would be lonely later that night.

Read 2 Samuel 11:2b
A Peeping David

Like women who visit a mikveh today, Bathsheba and the other women watched the sun disappear under the horizon. As the night sky darkened, stars appeared. When three stars twinkled down, they could bathe in the mikveh. Bathsheba and the other women were niddah or unclean, but once they performed the ancient ritual, they would emerge clean.

Perhaps, if only Uriah was home, she might have thought, *we could be together again as husband and wife. I am at my peak of fertility so we might conceive a child.*

"Your turn," said the attendant, motioning Bathsheba to enter the open-to-the-sky enclosure. Bathsheba opened her robe, then stepped out of her tunic. She loosened her hair and ran her fingers through it.

Bathsheba stepped down into the waist-high water still warm from the day's sunshine.

"*Barukh atah Ado-nai Elo-henu melekh ha'olam asher kideshanu b'mitzvotav v'tzivanu al ha'tevillah,*" she recited. (Blessed are You, O Lord, our God, King of the universe, who has sanctified us with His commandments and commanded us regarding the immersion.)

She held her breath and slid under.

Holding the torch over the water, the attendant checked to certify every part of Bathsheba—including every hair—was totally submerged.

Surfacing, Bathsheba shivered as the cool night air swept over her body. Intent on obeying God's command, she recited the blessing and immersed herself two more times.

Hidden by the night, a royal audience watched. God was watching, too.

The Palace on a Hill

To David, the Ark of the Covenant and supporting tabernacle was the crown jewel of his city. Bible scholars believe he placed the Ark near his new palace because he wanted the great blessings enjoyed by the last household who sheltered it.

David threw a big party as he brought in the Ark, which was to be housed in the tabernacle adjacent to his palace in the City of David. How important is this? (2 Samuel 6:2-15 and 2 Samuel 6:17, 18 paint a pretty clear picture of the layout and proximity of David's palace and the tabernacle where the mikveh were located.)

Very!

After the Ark was reinstated in the tent David erected, the devout could come to the tabernacle to pray and perform other acts of worship. Surrounding the tabernacle were multiple mikveh, some for men and some for women.

Herein is a significant clue to how David saw Bathsheba bathing.

Remember this: She came to the tabernacle to fulfill a sacred ritual obligation to her husband and God.

To those unfamiliar with this ritual, it may seem strange. Or slightly erotic. To Jews, it was a common practice. But to a king with no more giants to slay and a "who is going to tattle on me?" outlook, it evidently was a golden distraction.

Up on the Rooftop

From the roof he saw a woman bathing. The woman was very beautiful... (2 Sam. 11:2)

David couldn't sleep. Maybe it was a hot night. Maybe he was contemplating what riches his men would find when the treasure city of Rabbah fell. Maybe he had a fight with his first wife, Michel.

He paced the roof of his luxurious palace, stopping now and then to gaze over his city canopied by the fading sunset. From his high perch, he spotted a cluster of women near the mikveh. Among them was a stunningly beautiful woman about to bathe. David knew he should avert his eyes. But he had the perfect view.

(**Read 2 Samuel 11:3b — 4a**)

David sent someone to find out about her.

The man said, "She is Bathsheba, the daughter of Eliam and the wife of Uriah the Hittite."

Then David sent messengers to get her.

To better understand David's sense of entitlement, he was not accustomed to being denied anything he wanted. (**Read 2 Samuel 12:7b - 10**)

This is what the Lord, the God of Israel, says:

'I anointed you king over Israel, and I delivered you from the hand of Saul. [8]I gave your master's house to you, and your master's wives into your arms. I gave you all Israel and Judah. And if all this had been too little, I would have given you even more.

(**Read Psalm 139**)

Some people can't handle God's blessing and favor. It appears David was one of those.

He was so proud of his devotion to God. David challenged Him to see if any wickedness was in him. Despite God's personalized attention on David, when Bathsheba was observed worshipping God, all of David's self-righteous assertions of God's favor drowned in the mikveh. There was enough wickedness in David to take a friend's wife with his eyes wide open and eventually plot a murder.

As David was arranging pillows on his bed and lighting scented candles in preparation for Bathsheba's appearance, someone tapped David on the shoulder. In Iron Age vernacular, he asked, "Aren't you forgetting something?"

"Isn't this Bathsheba ... the wife of Uriah the Hittite?"

David apparently didn't care Uriah shared his privations when Saul was chasing David all over the countryside. David made his demand.

> *Then David sent messengers to get her.*
> (Read 2 Samuel 11:3b-4)
> *She came to him, and he slept with her.*

When a king summons you, you obey. You don't ask "Why?" or "Should I pack an overnight bag?" You just go.

As Bathsheba followed the messengers to the palace, we wonder what her thoughts were. Did she think something happened to her grandfather, father, and/or husband while in the king's service? Did she have a clue what the king wanted? Did the messengers hint her destination would be the king's bedroom? Afterwards, did she regret obeying the summons?

Or was she looking to have a fling with a king? (C)

Could Bathsheba Have Said, "No" to the King and Lived to Tell it?

Renaissance artists pictured Bathsheba as a seductress and David her innocent dupe.

On the other hand, some scholars focus on the phrase "... he took her," "took" being a word whose meaning indicates Bathsheba was raped or very nearly so — not a willing participant at all.

And when it came to pretty ladies in distress, David was not a complete lout — even if he put the damsel in distress himself. Case-in-point: Abigail became one of his wives after a rather nasty incident between David and her first husband. (1 Sam. 25)

We don't know if Bathsheba begged David to stop. We don't know if she said, "Think what you're doing!" We don't know if she tried to talk him out of it. But it doesn't much matter, as any argument Bathsheba might have made was ineffectual because we know how the night turned out.

There is an intriguing bit of cultural trivia that better explains God's anger with David over his tryst with Bathsheba — not that He didn't already have reason enough.

When Jewish husbands went off to war, they foresaw the possibility that they might die in battle. Recovery of the slain was a problem. Corpses were sometimes mutilated, decapitated, or set on fire. Without a body, a man could not be declared dead and there was not a statute of limitations on this technicality.

Responsible husbands left their wives a *get* (Talmud: *Shab.* 56a) or a conditional, retroactive divorce allowing a woman to be divorced and remarry if her husband did not return from war.[1]

---

[1] From the *Artscroll English Tanach*, the Jewish Bible with Insights from Classical Rabbinic Thought, "Technically, Bath-sheba (sic) could be considered an unmarried

However, at the time of the scandal, Bathsheba was not divorced. I believe Bathsheba was an alluring temptation *because* she was married. An adrenaline junkie, David craved a taste of forbidden fruit (2 Sam. 12: 8, 9). He wanted the excitement of sin.

Did David—or anyone—ask Bathsheba what she wanted?

A Royal Mess

The woman conceived and sent word to David, saying, "I am pregnant." (2 Sam. 11:3b-5 NIV)

Uh oh. David should have seen that coming.

Bathsheba also might have anticipated a visit from the stork.

Much of the remainder of David's life was consumed with trying to deal with the consequences of what he did to Bathsheba—which only made things worse.

His first plan was to confuse the timing of Bathsheba's pregnancy. He brought Uriah back from the war, got him drunk two nights in a row, then sent him home to Bathsheba. To David's frustration, a sloshed Uriah practiced more self-control than a sober David. Because of the prohibition against sex during times of war—abstaining from sex was supposed to make soldiers more aggressive—Uriah slept on the palace welcome mat and stayed battle-ready.

People were no different in Bathsheba's time than they are now. Whisper a rumor in any office today and the walls will repeat it. It probably wasn't long until Uriah knew the king had betrayed him.

Failing to persuade Uriah to sleep with Bathsheba, David contrived a murder-by-proxy scheme to maintain his choirboy image. Ironically, Uriah delivered his own death sentence. David not only had Uriah's blood on his hands, but also the blood of the soldiers under Uriah's command who were slaughtered, too.

If you can't be a good example, you can be a horrible warning. David's life proved to be a classic warning of the avalanche of the bad things set in motion when you sleep with a friend's wife and then arrange his murder.

Before everyone at court, David's sins of adultery, deception, and murder were boldly confronted by the prophet Nathan. Because David's sin was public, so was his punishment. (2 Sam. 12) David repented but his sons took advantage of his dip in popularity by fomenting rebellion against him. Although his fall was public and spectacular, God mercifully restored David to the throne. But the trust factor was broken. Who would want to serve as David's bodyguard ever again? Damage to David's

---

woman, for, as the Talmud (Shabbos56b) states, David's troops always gave their wives conditional divorces, lest a soldier be missing in action, leaving his wife unable to remarry.

reputation and reign was permanent.

In his lifetime, the sword never again left his house as his sons vied for power and their father's crown.

Three Funerals and a Wedding

Poor Bathsheba. Although David's drama is riveting, let's not overlook the price paid by the innocent woman at the heart of this tragedy.

The aftermath of sin is like dropping a bottle of India ink. Shards of glass go everywhere, black ink spatters on everything and you spend a lifetime cleaning it up. The innocent suffers. Bathsheba was painfully impacted by David's actions by losing one family member after another.

When Bathsheba discovered the conspiracy around Uriah's murder, it must have been a terrible revelation to her. What a crushing grief she must have felt as she mourned for her faithful husband.

Then David and Bathsheba's child was born. Their baby teetered between life and death. When her baby boy died, she was inconsolable although David tried.

Bathsheba's family turned against David. Ahithophel, her grandfather and David's chief advisor, backed David's son Absalom in a conspiracy to seize the throne from David. When the mutiny failed, Ahithophel committed suicide and Absalom was killed. (2 Sam. 15:12, 17:23) Another season of mourning for Bathsheba.

Can a Wrong Ever Be Right?

How did David's and Bathsheba's marriage turn out?

It began with illicit desire, rape, betrayal, and murder, then tried by trauma, trouble, and heartbreak. Bathsheba had ample reasons to be voted president emeritus of the I-hate-David club. Instead, she apparently accepted the situation, forgave him, and made the most of the mess.

Their marriage must have become a love match of some description because they had four more sons (1 Chron. 3:5). One of their sons, Solomon, was jumped ahead of his older half-brothers in line of succession to David's throne.

Although he was a wildly unpopular choice, Solomon eventually did succeed David, largely owing to Bathsheba's vigilance. Wise words whispered in her husband's ear saved both herself and Solomon from execution.

Sin poisons the sweetest well. But we have a God who recycles, a Redeemer who salvages ruined lives. Who can transform a rape into a marriage. Out of coal, He brings diamonds. Out of ashes, He brings beauty — but not without pain, both His and ours.

What Happened to Bathsheba? (A) (D)

In his writings, Proverbs, Ecclesiastes, and Song of Solomon, King Solomon credits his success as much to his mother's wise teaching as to his famous father's advice. Over and over, he counsels, "Listen to your mother."

Based on an oracle taught him by his mother, Solomon describes his idealized pattern for a wife (Pr. 31). Perhaps his search for a woman to live up to that ideal led Solomon to take 700 wives and 300 concubines.

How did Bathsheba make a success out of the marriage that began as an attack on her innocence? That robbed her of her beloved Uriah? That cost her first-born son?

It took the wisdom that spawned a Solomon, reputedly the wisest man who ever lived. Read his wisdom in Proverbs and follow the advice. Solomon should have taken his own advice.

Did beautiful Bathsheba become a woman who could extend forgiveness and grace to the one whose actions changed the trajectory of her life? Yes, in return for painful lessons as a grievously wronged woman, she became the archetype for the Virtuous Woman. (Pr. 31)

Debates about her guilt or innocence continue, her reputation still takes a beating. Sin always demands a price.

Bathsheba discovered blessings bathe the woman who lives life guided by God's wisdom. Drops of mercy from hard-learned wisdom are apparent through her ability to forgive David, resulting in a tender marriage and her son Solomon's ascendance to his father's throne.

From the pages of Proverbs, her wisdom inspires the misused, abused, sin-tarnished, and brokenhearted.

May godly wisdom empower you to make the most of any bad situation in your life, too.

Let's talk about Bathsheba —

A. When a marriage or life begins on the wrong foot, how can God help it get back on track?
B. Uriah, Bathsheba's first husband, appears to be a loving, honorable man and soldier, devoted to his wife. David had fame, riches, and several wives. Why do you think some women find wealth, power, fame, and talent more desirable than committed love?
C. The author's view is that Bathsheba was raped with no choice in the matter. What's your opinion? Could Bathsheba have said no and lived to tell it?
D. How does following godly wisdom help repair a damaged reputation?
E. Has this study changed your perception of Bathsheba? Why and how? Or not.

Just Between You and God

Have you been the victim of a crime? Has someone you respected betrayed you? Ask God how He can help you turn it into a blessing for you and others. (2 Sam. 11:2)

Chapter Five
The Wise Woman of Tekoah:
She Used Her Talent to Heal a Family and Nation

Another visit to Israel ...

En Dor — I am excited to visit this Galilean kibbutz for many reasons. Long ago, on what was to be the last night of his life, King Saul consulted a witch here (1 Samuel 28) and received a prophecy of a disastrous battle.

But on this night, in the soft winter twilight, I do not expect to encounter a witch. Nor a prophecy of war. Rather, the women here are sowing seeds of peace.

Around an open brazier to ward off the night's chill, with cups of hot mint-scented tea in hand, Jewish, Arab Muslim, Christian, and Circassian woman and their children tell traditional folktales. As the storytelling begins, children from thumb-sucking babes to teenagers to newly minted military draftees stick close to their mothers and grandmothers. But as the evening wears on, the children forget their differences. Little ones share small toys with others. The older kids exchange shy smiles. Regardless of race or religion, they lock eyes in understanding as they share the jokes or pathos in the narratives.

The real magic occurs among the adult women. Centuries-old religious, political, and cultural differences melt away when they are caught up together in the drama and romance of the stories. Will the young lovers escape the grasp of the evil rich king and live happily ever after? Will the brother in exile save his family? Will the little shepherdess find the lost goat?

The kibbutz is in an area of Israel where clashes of cultures and religions might cause tension. But they don't — due in large part to the storytelling.

One of the women organizers of the storytelling nights explains why sharing folktales brings understanding between conflicting peoples: "All of us have a common past in the Land. Our stories have common threads in the locality as workers in agriculture and as fellow human beings. Understanding each other's folktales helps us appreciate their religion and culture."

Begun with the telling of tales, the women cooperate in collective projects like making olive oil by old-time methods and learning each other's traditional crafts. Tonight, they will make necklaces of olive wood and leather, deeply symbolic of extending an olive branch of peace to one another. But there is an ancient tie that binds them together — the shared bloodline of Abraham. They are, after all, family.

Further, the organizer tells me that the women have become involved in each other's lives, sending cards and notes, and visiting. Children become friends. Long-held animosities slowly disappear.

These women are changing perceptions, one story at a time. They may have taken their cue from a story told by the Wise Woman of Tekoah.

Changing Perceptions, One Story at a Time

Who — or what — can bring reconciliation when a feud divides not only the ruling family but also the nation?

Family squabbles are always tricky to mediate. What sort of person uses words that heal and unite?

A very wise woman.

We don't know her actual name, but we'll call her Jada, meaning "wise" in Hebrew.

What we do know is from the little village of Tekoah, an amazing woman stepped forward to use her storytelling talent to hold up a mirror so the king could plainly see himself and his situation.

Who was Jada, this wise woman of Tekoah? What story did she tell? What did it mean? Why should we care?

Amazingly, when we look at what we can discover about this wise woman of Tekoah, we will find that her story holds a secret message for us, too.

An Ancient "Daytime Drama"

The ongoing feud in King David's court reads like a soap opera summary.

It began with a sordid, illicit, one-sided love affair. David's son Amnon fell in love with his beautiful half-sister Tamar and raped her. David did nothing. His own actions with Bathsheba had cost him his moral authority. (A) (B)

Outraged, the princess's brother, Absalom, gave up waiting on his father to discipline Amnon and took vengeance into his hands, slaughtering Amnon. Then ran. For three years, Absalom lived in exile.

As chief mourner, father of the guilty perpetrator, judge, and jury, David vacillated. And suffered. With his own actions festering in his conscience, how could he fairly judge this situation?

For once, Israel was at peace with its enemies — albeit an uneasy peace. On every side, secretly rebellious factions looked for chinks in David's armor. For the king to be distracted was a real danger to the country.

The entire nation was watching to see what David would do. Everyone had an opinion. Some thought Absalom should be punished: some admired him for acting. (C)

There were questions about King David's ability to effectively govern since he had apparently lost control of his own family.

Moreover, whole regions of the country had taken sides.

Joab, the commander of David's army, realized if this situation wasn't quickly resolved, the sides would turn on each other and civil war would result. (D)

A Plot to Bring Peace (2 Samuel 14)
Joab puzzled how he could comfort his friend and king yet squeeze a decision out of him before a civil war broke out. A seasoned warrior and military strategist, he understood how David thought.

The two men had so much history. Joab stood with David when former King Saul was chasing David all over the desert. Joab was there when David was crowned king and helped vanquish his numerous enemies. He unquestioningly sent their longtime comrade-at-arms Uriah the Hittite on the suicide mission. Now, three years following the murder of Amnon, it pained Joab to see David still mourning. This time for his son Absalom.

Absalom had taken sanctuary with his grandfather Talmai, King of Geshur. If Absalom came back to Israel, perhaps the situation would resolve itself. (D)

Here is how I imagine this encounter occurred: Joab's gaze rested on the hill marking Tekoah. The village had a master storyteller. Her tales were like magic carpets, sweeping hearers away to strange lands and curious accounts. At the end of her stories, she would shoot an arrow of God's truth into the heart of every member of her audience.

Could she, would she, use her talent to give the king perspective on what he should do with Absalom?

The woman of Tekoah agreed with Joab. It was time to do something to bring healing to a king, his family and nation.

Wisdom's Magic Carpet
In Proverbs, Solomon repeatedly urges readers to seek wisdom. As defined by scripture, godly wisdom is multifaceted.

One facet of wisdom is knowing how to manage your God-given talents for good. Biblical wisdom weaves natural raw talent with learning, discipline, good sense, God sense, balance, timing, and action. True godly wisdom will take you to heights you only dreamed of achieving; however, they are the heights you were born to achieve.

Another facet of biblical wisdom involves maintaining a balance between the opposite extremes embedded in one's personality and the extremes that present themselves throughout life. Solomon addressed these extremes in Ecclesiastes 3: "There is a time for everything, and a season for every activity under heaven: a time to be born and a time to die, a time to plant and a time to uproot, a time to kill and a time to heal…" (1-3a)

Godly wisdom contains the ability to know when to do what. Because only God knows the future, wisdom dictates we pray over every aspect of when and how to use your talents.

But King David was not all Psalms and harps. He was a man of war. Suppose he took offense at Jada's message? And what if he took it out on the messenger?

Catching the King by the Tale

Jada costumed herself as a grieving mother to tell her most important story. Turning the neckline tear of her sackcloth tunic this way and that, she finally positioned it so her chest would be modestly covered yet the torn fabric could be plainly seen. Pushing away lotions, she removed her veil, bunched her hair into wild tangles and sprinkled dust upon her head. As a final touch, she removed her shoes and distorted her face until she looked the embodiment of fresh grief. (Ez. 24:17)

As she prepared, Joab paced outside Jada's house. This was going to be tricky. He had concocted a believable story, something close to the king's actual predicament but not so close as to immediately arouse David's suspicion.

As they travelled the twelve miles to the City of David, he educated her on the situation inside the palace. Depending on how David reacted and what questions he asked, she would be required to think on her feet.

Once inside the palace, Jada joined the long line of supplicants presenting their cases before the king.

She studied David, watching him for clues to his mood. He was older now, his golden-red hair shot with silver, his skin weathered by the sun. He appeared tired, distracted, as if he had lost interest in his people. She knew it would take all her skill to capture and hold David's attention.

When it was her turn to present her case, she stepped before his throne and fell face first. "Help me, O king!"

David held up his jewel-encrusted hand. The hubbub in the throne room ceased.

"What is troubling you?"

"My lord, my husband is dead. I, your servant, had two sons. Out in the field, they fought. No one was there to separate them. One struck the other and killed him."

Sighing heavily, she continued. "My whole clan has revolted against me, saying, 'Hand over the son who killed his brother. We will execute him for his crime, then we will get rid of the heir as well.'"

She paused to allow her final statement to make full impact.

"They wish to extinguish the only burning coal I have left. My late husband will have neither name nor descendant on the earth!"

"Go home. I will issue an order in your behalf."

The king turned to the scribe to dictate his command.

"Please, my lord, let me take his punishment! Put his blame on my father's family. You and your throne can be without guilt."

The king paused in his dictation. "If anyone gives you trouble, bring him to me. He will not bother you again."

"Let the king invoke the LORD God to prevent vengeance from adding to the destruction, so that my son will not be executed."

David was growing impatient. "As the LORD lives, your son will not lose a hair."

Suddenly, Jada the storyteller of Tekoah stood boldly before the king. "As your servant, may I speak a word to my lord the king?"

David was astonished. "All right. Speak."

"Aren't you punishing God's children? Aren't you convicting yourself? You have not brought back your banished son. Water spilled on the ground cannot be recovered, so we die. But God does not throw away a life. Instead, He devises ways the banished can be reconciled to Him.

"I told you the tale of my sons because you are like an angel of God discerning good and evil. Now, may God be with you."

Jada turned to leave.

"Wait! I want an answer! Is the hand of Joab with you in all this?"

Stunned silence filled the throne room.

Go Home

So, what happened to Jada, King David, and Joab?

David saw wisdom in Jada's words. He brought Absalom home to Jerusalem. Unfortunately, the family drama continued. David and Absalom's actions fomented rebellion and deepened national divisions. (Read 2 Samuel 14:13-14)

The wise, all-knowing God does not make that mistake. Before the first brother killed his sibling in a jealous rage, God planned a way to reconcile with the banished. He always wants to bring the outcast home.

For all who gaze into the night skies and ask, "God, can You forgive me? Will You forgive me? I've committed such terrible sins," the wise

47

woman of Tekoah explicitly gives you the answer you seek: "As water spilled on the ground cannot be recovered, we die. But God does not throw away a life. Instead, He devises ways the banished can be reconciled to Him."

"Come home," He says to the murderer, thief, liar, gambler, adulterer—all of us. "It's true: your actions caused My Son to be murdered. But I don't want to lose you, too."

Out of the pages of the Bible steps the wise woman of Tekoah. She has a message for you: "Go home. Your Father is waiting to welcome you."

Let's Talk About the Wise Woman of Tekoah

A. David felt unable to pronounce judgment on his son Absalom for killing his brother because of his own sin in arranging the death of Bathsheba's husband along with his men. What kind of actions or situations can cause a parent to lose moral authority?
B. How do you think David should have responded to his daughter's rape by her brother? What punishment fits the crime?
C. Absalom waited for David to do something. When he didn't, Absalom took revenge by killing his brother. Is vigilante justice ever warranted?
D. Sometimes a person is too close to a problem to properly address it. What can you do to help someone gain perspective on their situation?
E. What characteristics do you look for in a wise person?

Just Between You and God

Ask God how to wisely use the talent or gifts He has given you. Ask Him what steps you should take to maximize it to fulfill His purpose for loaning it to you.

Chapter Six
The Widow of Zarephath:
She Fed Her Family on Faith

A single pita—that was all that stood between the widow of Zarephath and starvation.

No public assistance. No food pantry. No generous benefactor. Her community and neighbors couldn't help. They were on the verge of starvation, too.

Unless God intervened, the widow and her son would suffer the same outcome. Because she was stronger, she would have to watch him fade away before she, too, died.

Yet somehow in a land dominated by Jezebel's pagan worship, a Canaanite widow miraculously discovered a secret storehouse of hope: her newfound faith in God. (A)

In times of crisis, some blame God. She chose to look to Him for help.

I imagine this widow had sins from her past that clouded her hope in God. If she could undo the past or make amends, she would. She hoped—prayed—He would forgive.

As with other women in the Bible, the widow's given name is not recorded, but we will call her Nediva, meaning "noble and generous" in Hebrew. Jesus mentions her in a pantheon of the unlikely faithful. Nediva, a single mother desperately trying to keep her child alive during a food crisis, did something incredibly noble and generous. Or what some would call foolish. She trusted God and gave away her last pita.

How did she know this was what God wanted her to do and not her own foolish notion? How did God speak to her? How can we clearly hear God during a crisis? Will God bless a person with a sordid past?

The answers are contained in the story of the widow of Zarephath.

Making Dough

On one of my visits to Israel, the aroma of baking bread wafts through the open-air market in a Druze village on the slopes of Mount Carmel. An elderly woman colorfully dressed in traditional clothing, her face a tracery of smile lines, is baking flatbread the old-fashioned way—on a wok-like iron skillet inverted over a charcoal fire.

The recipe is stored in her memory, but she tells it to me: half unbleached white flour and half whole wheat flour, salt, water, a little oil, and yeast. Stir together and set to rising two hours in advance of baking.

She takes a lump of dough, deftly pats it into a thin pancake, then flips it on the skillet where it freckles as it heats. A quick flip to toast the other side and the bread is done. Start to finish, the bread bakes in minutes over a modest amount of fuel. Surprisingly sustaining, the bread is eaten plain, topped with salty herbs, or filled with any one of traditional fillings.

But if only one piece of flat bread stood between your family and starvation, then God told you to give it away, could you? Would you?

What kind of woman was Nediva, the widow of Zarephath, who could? And did.

In the Raven's Haven

(Read 1 Kings 17:1-9)

Elijah studied the horizon as he waited for the arrival of the ravens. Would they feed him today? As the sky pinked and the birds did not come, he suspected God was about to give him new instructions. Hunger made him listen.

He still thought it strange God sent ravens—the most unlikely of waitstaff—to feed him twice a day. God was telling him something by using the ravens, but he couldn't put together the pieces.

He mused over what he knew about ravens: They were ritually unclean for Jews and so to be avoided. Yet God sent them to feed him. Ravens might not even feed their own hatchlings, but they faithfully fed him.

A phrase from Moses' writing kept flittering in his brain: "Noah... sent out a raven from the ark, and it kept flying back and forth until the water had dried up from the earth." (Gen. 8:7)

Elijah felt he was in an ark of safety. King Ahab and Jezebel were looking for him. Yet they couldn't find him in his plain sight hiding place.

The sun was fully up before Elijah concluded the ravens weren't coming. He went to the brook for a drink. The water was dried up.

God was about to send him elsewhere. When the Word of God spoke to his spirit, He was specific: "Leave now. Go to Zarephath of Sidon and stay there. In Zarephath, I have commanded a widow to supply you with food." (1 Kings 17:9)

Elijah laughed. He recognized God's leading was being relayed to him wrapped in the joke. The ravens who fed him were both the leading and confirmation since a Gentile waitress was as unlikely—some would say unsuitable—as a raven. And the drinkable water had dried up.

How would he recognize the widow when he saw her? Would she look like a raven? (In Acts 10, read how God used a similar object lesson to guide Peter.)

"Hello. God? Is That You?"

Would you like to have a conversation with God? He would like to have a chat with you. In fact, He is speaking to you now. Listen.

What? Do you doubt that He is speaking because you don't hear Him with your ears? He speaks with many voices. There are other parts of you that hear too.

Just because we cannot hear a certain sound doesn't mean it is not there. Depending upon the breed, dogs hear sounds — whistles and far distant sirens, even ultrasound waves — we simply cannot since their hearing is twice as acute as ours.

Think about it: Right now, radio, television, and wireless Internet waves are passing through your body. Rap music, reruns of *Lassie*, cell phone conversations, secret government transmissions, all are swirling around and through you, unseen and unheard — unless you have a receiver tuned to the right frequency.

It is the same with the voice of God. He is speaking. Now. Can you hear Him? Is your spiritual receiver on? Are you tuned to the right frequency? Are you open to hearing from Him?

Elijah heard Him. The widow of Zarephath heard Him. Billions of others have heard Him. You can hear Him, too. Stay tuned. (B)

A Strange Place to Hide

So, he (Elijah) arose and went to Zarephath. And when he came to the gate of the city, indeed a widow was there gathering sticks... (1 Kings 17:10a, NKJV)

Hunger-pinched faces of children. Skinny little arms and legs. As Elijah traveled north to Zarephath, he saw people scavenging. He was distressed that God had sent ravens to feed him while little children cried because their stomachs were empty.

As Elijah approached Zarephath, the number of starving people grew. *Which widow is the right widow? How strange God would hide me from the most powerful woman in the region by hiding me in the home of one of the most powerless. And in Jezebel's home country, too.*

Where Faith Grows Wild

Here's a head-scratcher: Faith in God sometimes blooms in rocky patches where it seems unlikely it could take root and grow, such as in a hospital where a young mother is dying of a wasting disease. Or in a back alley where a ten-year-old girl is aborting her rapist's child. Or in a prison cell on death row.

Faith in God may be withered and diseased — even dead — where you would expect it to be thriving.

Jesus commented on this phenomenon when, near the height of His fame, He returned to Nazareth. To the hometown folks, He was simply Jesus, the local carpenter. Everyone acknowledged His carpentry skill, but He certainly was no one special. "So He heals—so what? Yes, He makes water into wine. Doesn't every carpenter?"

Their snide comments reminded Jesus of the widow of Zarephath:

"No prophet is accepted in his hometown," Jesus observed. "There were many widows in Israel in Elijah's time, during which there was a severe famine throughout the land. Yet Elijah was not sent to any of them, but to a widow in Zarephath." (Lk. 4:24–26 paraphrase)

As an unlikely believer flourishing in a harsh environment, nevertheless Nediva trusted God. Although Scripture doesn't say when exactly she came to faith in the God of Israel, I imagine the drought and famine had caused her to doubt the Canaanite gods she had been raised to worship. She had questions, and some basic faith by the time God chose her to shelter Elijah. Her faith in Him wasn't superficial: she trusted Him to death. And God blessed her.

How does such a faith grow and thrive? How do we fertilize our faith when things are good, so it is strong in days of famine? Nediva knew. Now you can know, too.

Trusting to Death
(1 Kings 17: 10–16)

At least we still have water, Nediva thought as she deposited her little son in the shadow of the town walls, placing the newly filled water jug next to him. Shading her eyes, she searched for twigs to make a fire to cook a final meal.

She was hungry. Her little boy was hungry. She had spun out her meager supplies as far as they would stretch. As her stores dwindled, Nediva looked to God to answer her desperate prayers. As of today, there was only enough flour and oil left for a single cake. Then, she guessed, they would die—unless God intervened.

Nediva didn't know a great deal about the God of Israel. What she did know, however, was that He was a good God, not thirsty for the blood of babies and children like her native gods. That, among other things, convinced her to trust and worship Him.

As the drought continued, she no doubt heard that Elijah, the famous prophet of Israel, was to blame. King Ahab was pursuing Elijah with murderous intent. Ahab had long arms and many spies. Perhaps during those years of dwindling water and food, soldiers came through the village, vainly searching for Elijah.

Zarephath was in Queen Jezebel's home territory. Their lives would be in grave danger if Elijah was found anywhere nearby. Perhaps Elijah was in Nediva's thoughts that day. Perhaps she had a strange notion that God would want her to help the prophet, if he did come to the village.

Nediva told God, "If it's You that is asking, send the prophet. I'll care for him as best as I can."

Moments later, maybe she laughed at herself for imagining God spoke to her. After all, who was she? And they were hungry.

Her arms were nearly full of twigs when a dusty traveler spoke to her.

"Would you bring me a little water in a jar so I may have a drink?"

Nediva looked up and a thrill ran through her as she identified his accent.

He's Jewish. Could this be...? she wondered, thinking back to her imagining of just moments ago.

She nodded. As she stepped to fetch the water jug, he called to her again.

"And bring me, please, a piece of bread."

She dropped the twigs. "As surely as the LORD your God lives, I don't have any bread — only a handful of flour in a jar and a little oil in a jug. I am gathering these few sticks to take home and make a meal for my son and myself and then die."

"Don't be afraid," the stranger said. Was she hallucinating, from hunger or thirst? Could he be Elijah? Had God been speaking to her? "Go home. Do as you have planned. But first make a small cake of bread for me from what little you have and bring it to me. Then make something for yourself and your son. This is what the LORD, the God of Israel, says: 'Your jar of flour will not empty, nor will the jug of oil run dry until the day the LORD gives rain on the land.'"

Nediva stared at the traveler. He was asking to share their meal. Was this man Elijah, Israel's prophet of God? Or was her little boy about to be cheated out of his final meal?

She decided to trust God. And the consequences were beyond her imagination.

"Let Me Repeat Using Small Words," Saith the Lord

Trusting God is often counter-intuitive. We must battle our selfish nature to obey Him. Our mind says, "Be greedy," while God says, "Give." Our instinct is to hoard when He says, "Share." We want to look out for Number One when He says, "Look to Me."

But He knows that. However, He speaks very clearly to those actively listening. To be certain we don't miss His message, He'll repeat it two or three times in various ways. (2 Cor. 13:1)

He has many imaginative ways to verify you are hearing His voice. Sometimes, a godly friend will confirm what He is urging you to do.

Circumstances may line up. Sometimes He'll speak through a book or sermon. He's been known to open a door, shove you through it, and slam it behind you.

The Holy Spirit will never tell you to do something in clear disagreement with the Word of God. (Jn. 15:26) If you think you're supposed to marry an unbeliever, have an affair, or get naked at the airport, it wasn't God who put those ideas in your mind.

You are free to be skeptical. Be cautious and wise. 1 John 4:1 instructs us to "try" or test "the spirits whether they are of God: because many false prophets are gone out into the world."

Practice listening to Him daily. Read His Word, then ask, "What do You want to say to me through this Scripture? Is there anything You want me to do? To say? Change?" You'll soon learn to recognize His voice.

Somehow, some way, God "commanded" Nediva. She heard Him and her adventure began.

Recipe for Miracles

A jar of flour. A jug of oil. Both nearly empty.

Before Nediva could change her mind, she quickly emptied the containers into her mixing bowl and made the bread. As it toasted over the fire, her son hungrily sniffed the air.

"After we take this bread to the prophet, I'll make you some," she promised him.

Please, God, she prayed in her heart as she carried the bread to the prophet, *please provide.*

Back at her firepit, Nediva shook the flour jar. Minutes before, she had emptied it, but now... She shook the jar over the bowl. A cascade of flour poured out. She reached for the oil jug. It was strangely heavy. She tipped it. A rivulet of golden oil plowed a path through the flour.

The next day, it happened again. And the next. And the next. And the next. Every day was a miracle.

Why is God so good to me? She was humbled and amazed.

But in the back of Nediva's mind, a worry niggled: What would happen if God remembered her sins and decided to punish her? Would He suddenly turn angry and vengeful—like Baal?

Baal? Jehovah? Aren't All Gods Good?

You judge.

Some form of "Baal" was included in the name of many ancient gods or idols. We know only bits and pieces about Baal as worshipped by King Ahab and his queen Jezebel, daughter of the king of Sidon, the land where Zarephath is located. (1 Kings 16:29–33)

Here's what we know:

Baal was a fertility god, worshipped as the bringer of rain and crop productivity. As such, sexual immorality and prostitution was part of worship.

Sexual servitude is never part of the worship of God. He is worshipped in spirit and truth. (Jn. 4:24) And purity.

To prove that the Lord God was the real provider while Baal was only a figment of an evil imagination, the Word of God came to Elijah to decree no rain or dew would fall without his say-so. (1 Kings 17:1) And the skies obediently dried up.

Throughout the drought, God provided for those who worshipped Him.

Baal was also worshipped as the source of national prosperity.

These practices were only the beginning of ritual Baal worship God found so abhorrent. Child sacrifice was widespread and dominant. (C) (D)

Beginning with Abraham, the God of Israel decisively made known His opposition to child sacrifice. (Gen. 22)

God also takes it as a personal affront when children are abused (Lk. 15:2) and advocates for the fatherless child. (Ps. 10:14)

Here is something else uniquely remarkable about the God of the Bible: He knows your name.

You may hear worshippers of other gods say, "I love _____ (fill in your choice). But you never hear them say, "My god loves me." He doesn't know them. They are nameless, faceless, and unimportant unless they do something – blow themselves up or sacrifice their child – to capture their god's attention.

The God of the Bible not only knows your name and face, but also the details of your life down to the number of hairs on your head. (Lk. 12:7)

So you choose which god – or God – to serve, worship, and obey.

Nediva chose. And reaped in ways she could not have guessed. As she continued to feed Elijah, the flour and oil continued to divinely regenerate in the jars. The more she heard about the God of Israel, the more she realized that she had once been duped. Baal was only an idol. And death.

Hanging over her head were the sins of her past, her days of worshipping Baal. Haunted by it, she was sick with fear.

Horror Of Sin
(1 Kings 17: 17–24)

Nediva saw the statue of Baal in her sleep. Glowing, with blood-red flames shooting out of his open maw, he laughed at her. Then he showed her scenes of her past life as his worshipper.

"Your new God knows what you have done," he taunted. "Will He forgive? No! Now give me your son and you can return to me."

Nediva awoke, drenched with sweat. The God she now served was a living God. And life.

Yet the dreams persisted along with memories of her past sins. She thought about confessing all to Elijah and found some peace in that idea.

The prophet slept above her in the upper room. Why wasn't that enough to keep away the nightmares?

To reassure herself, she reached for her son, sleeping curled against her. She put her hand on his forehead. Fever! As the night wore on and morning light illuminated the mountains, she sponged him off, pleading with God to spare her son.

Instead, the child's fever soared as another punishing, rainless day dawned. Dust rolled off the parched ground and anyone who had any flour at all found it embedded with grit from the fields.

Nediva was panic-stricken, almost irrational with fear for her sick child. *If Elijah is a man of God, why doesn't he do something to save my son? What if his God is punishing me?*

Elijah paced the house as Nediva held her little boy, mopping his forehead as his fever climbed. His small chest rose and fell with increasing difficulty. Finally, it stopped.

Nediva screamed. "What do you have against me, man of God? Did you come to remind me of my sin and kill my son?"

"Give him to me." Elijah took the lifeless boy from her arms. Weeping, she slumped to the floor as the prophet carried her child upstairs to his room.

The prophet's voice echoed in the chamber above her, reverberating in her soul. "O LORD my God, have You brought tragedy also upon this widow by causing her son to die? O LORD, let this boy's life return to him!"

All was still except for Nediva's weeping and Elijah's footfalls on the stairs.

"Mama!"

Startled, Nediva looked up. Her son smiled.

"Look! Your son is alive!" Elijah said. He placed the boy in her arms.

"Now I know that you are a man of God and that the Word of the LORD is the truth!" she declared.

Recipe for Relationship

Flour and oil—the ingredients for life-sustaining bread. Trust and obedience—the ingredients for a life-giving relationship with God, no matter how impossible the circumstances.

A single pita — or five loaves and two small fishes — when mixed with trust and obedience becomes a banquet in His hands.

The widow of Zarephath found the secret for survival and a relationship with God — trust in Him and obedience to His Word.

Let's Talk About the Widow

A. Although Nediva was not a Jewess, God asked her to exercise great faith. Share your story of how you came to faith in Jesus.
B. Do you think God still speaks? Can you tell of a time you "heard" God's voice?
C. Baal demanded the sacrifice of infants and children to bring prosperity. Today, babies are routinely slaughtered in the womb for a variety of reasons, one of which is for economic advancement. What would you say to a woman contemplating an abortion?
D. What type of cruel false gods do you see worshipped today?
E. God did a miracle for Nediva and fed her during a famine. Has God ever provided for you in a miraculous way? Share your story.
F. Jesus found Nediva's faith to be remarkable. What do you find outstanding about her?

Just Between You and God

Is there something in your past that haunts you? Do you need to make restitution for something you have done? Ask God to lead you to scripture verses that pertain to your past situation.

Chapter Seven
Mary of Nazareth:
What Did it Cost Her to be God's
Handmaiden?

Picture this: Your thirteen-year-old daughter is pregnant.

She says, "The baby's father is God. And by the way, I'm still a virgin."

Stretches your ability to believe her, doesn't it?

I suspect Mary of Nazareth's parents would understand. (A)

While she is probably the most famous woman in the New Testament, Mary of Nazareth may also be the least understood. Volumes have been written on her life, while her name is mentioned less than thirty times in the entire canonical Bible. Yet, her story is bedrock to the Gospels.

Is it possible to sort out truth from legend regarding Mary of Nazareth?

Even with scant mention, Scripture is intent on impressing certain facts about Mary into our minds. First and foremost: Mary of Nazareth is the only human parent of Jesus Christ.

Which raises yet another question: Why are there two detailed genealogies of Jesus? What — if anything — do these family trees have to do with God choosing Mary to be the mother of the Messiah?

Then there are obvious questions about the birth of Jesus: Is a "virgin birth" possible? Did Mary concoct a tale to prevent being stoned to death as an adulteress, the common punishment for out-of-wedlock pregnancy in the first century? What does the Bible say about Mary's relationship with Joseph? Why did they journey to Bethlehem so close to Jesus' birth? Could a heavily pregnant woman travel ninety miles from Nazareth to Bethlehem?

We will visit Nazareth, the site of Jesus' conception and Mary's hometown. We will explore ancient texts to separate biblical truth from legends.

We will explore yet another, more obscure side to Mary of Nazareth's complex life. Only Mary could have known many of the details of Luke 2, so we can assume that information came directly from her. As hard as her story is to believe, something in it resonates to the depths of our souls, to our very cells. A spark springs to life that says, "A peasant girl didn't make this up. This is truth." What is it?

From her story, we'll learn what it truly means to invite Jesus to live in us, as we explore the life and calling of Mary of Nazareth and the ancient secrets of this woman of the Bible.

Nazareth — The Rose of Galilee

There is some scholarly tail-chasing on the meaning of Nazareth, but the earliest known is "shoot" or "sprout." The modern Hebrew word *nazar* means "rose" and has led tourist brochures to promote Nazareth as "The Rose of Galilee."

But when told that Jesus the Messiah hailed from there, Nathaniel quipped, "Can anything good come out of Nazareth?" This suggests the burg wasn't the pick of the garden in Jesus' day. (Jn. 1:46)

Why, then, would Mary and Joseph's families have chosen Nazareth as the place to rear their families?

It certainly wasn't for the building materials. Limestone in the Nazareth Ridge is the poorest in the entire region. Some suggest — quite reasonably — that Mary and Joseph were poverty-stricken settlers who couldn't afford to live in the nicer nearby towns where work could easily be had.

In short, the Nazareth of Jesus' day was likely the regional slum. Perched on the cusp of the beautiful Jezreel Valley (also known as the Valley of Armageddon), Nazareth was not and is not on any main trade routes. But it was a window on the world and witness to the parade of international travelers heading north and south.

Today, Nazareth is a pretty city with a robust economy fed by nearby farms and high-tech industries. Steeply twisting but picturesque streets make good brakes an absolute necessity. Unlike most towns in Israel and the West Bank, there has been very little archeological digging down under those streets. Any ancient sites were found by accident.

Until recently. In 2000, Nazareth Village, a recreation of first century Nazareth, uncovered an authentic winepress dating from Mary's day, putting to rest the debate whether anyone lived in Nazareth in Mary's time. In this recreated site, we get a sense of ancient Nazareth and what Mary's life was like, based mostly on written documents from the first century and other archeological digs.

Since the biblical account of Mary's life begins with the appearance of the angel Gabriel, what is the origin of all the stories about her early life? In sorting truth from fiction, certain facts emerge that may change how you view the mother of Christ.

Inquiring Minds Wanted to Know

Ever wonder what Jesus was like as a little kid? Other than that incident in the temple when He was a preteen (Lk. 2:41-32), did Mary ever have to curb His extraordinary abilities? Or was He just like any other little boy? Did something happen to alert Him that He was the Son of God? Or did He always know?

How about Mary's life? How did she come to be chosen as the handmaiden of God? Did others realize that she was highly favored by God? How did Mary's parents react to her claim that Jesus was conceived by the action of the Holy Spirit?

Want to know? Early believers did, too.

Luke, the author of the Gospel by the same name, gives us important clues to the answers in his preface:

Many have undertaken to draw up an account of the things that have been fulfilled among us, just as they were handed down to us by those who from the first were eyewitnesses and servants of the word. Therefore, since I myself have carefully investigated everything from the beginning, it seemed good also to me to write an orderly account for you, most excellent Theophilus, so that you may know the certainty of the things you have been taught. (Lk. 1:1-4 NIV)

The premise of the fictional *The DaVinci Code* is based on the idea that there existed additional gospel manuscripts. On this point, the *Code* and Luke agree. Lot of manuscripts from the second and third centuries exist about Mary and Jesus. Some contain fanciful, unsubstantiated stories, often contradicting the others. Knowledgeable eyewitnesses of the day judged these writings to be unreliable. (B)

Somewhere between 50-100 AD, Luke, a Gentile, and physician (Col. 4:14), compiled a factual case history on Jesus, Mary, and the extraordinary events surrounding them. He compiled his report from confirmed eyewitness accounts to send to Theophilus, a man some think was a high Roman official.

Luke does not embellish these stories. His purpose is to strip off sentimental claptrap, commentary spin, and report just the facts.

With an eye for detail, an ear for dialogue, and landmark dating, Luke's gospel is a carefully written scholarly account. Although versions exist telling tales of Mary's conception, her early life, as well as the upbringing of a precocious (smart-mouthed and very naughty!) little Jesus, we'll stick with Luke's gospel for facts.

Extraordinary facts they are.

Son of King David, Mary, God, and ?

Many eyes glaze over when reading "the begats" or Bible passages recounting family trees. But when you become familiar with Bible characters, genealogies are fascinating reading, like condensed bios of

your graduating class. For example, three other women in this study —
Rahab, Bathsheba, and Ruth — plus Mary are found in Jesus' family tree.

What are we to make of Jesus' family tree, especially since the
Matthew 1 genealogy varies from the record in Luke 3? A variety of
explanations — some ingenious, some silly — have been offered. The
simplest is the one I like best: There is no word for son-in-law in ancient
Hebrew.

Keeping that in mind, the reason for two records become rational.
Jesus was thought to be the son of Joseph. Joseph's family tree is in
Matthew. Mary's family tree is in Luke and Joseph is the son-in-law of
Heli. The two trees converge at Jesus.

Jesus' family trees are important because they prove Him to be
human and the heir of the throne of David. But why is Jesus "the Son of
God"?

A Messenger with Wings (C)

Armed Roman soldiers strutted down Nazareth's streets as though
they owned them. In more than one way, they did. Rome was the master;
Israel was their unwilling slave. Foreign invaders were one more outrage
Israel must bear until Messiah would deliver them and sit on the throne
of David.

As never before, every new mother in Israel from David's lineage
anxiously searched the face of her newborn son, hoping against hope her
baby might be the Messiah. His nation awaited Him to throw off Rome's
heavy boot.

As a betrothed woman, Mary covered her face while clandestinely
watching the soldiers. Suddenly, a very tall, very bright man stepped out
of the shadows. He was larger, more powerful than the soldiers. Without
armor, he glowed like the sun.

"Greetings, you who are highly favored! The Lord is with you!"

Mary blanched. What kind of greeting was this?

"Do not be afraid," he told her. "I am Gabriel."

Mary recognized him from the Scriptures. Gabriel was the angel
dispatched from God to the prophet Daniel (chapters 8 and 9) when
Babylon held Israel captive. This very angel foretold Israel's deliverance.

"Mary, you have found favor with God," he told her. "You will be
with Child and give birth to a Son, and you are to give Him the name
Jesus. He will be great and will be called the Son of the Most High. The
Lord God will give Him the throne of His father David, and He will reign
over the house of Jacob forever; His kingdom will never end."

Questions raced through Mary's mind. She did not doubt the bright
being's identity or message — although it astonished her to think that God
was mindful of her in her lowly status as a woman. (Lk. 1:48)

"How will this be?" Mary asked the angel. "I am a virgin."

Can a virgin conceive? This was — and is — a question worth asking.

The Birds and the Bees and the Christmas Tree

Yes, a physiological virgin can conceive. But that wasn't what Mary was asking. She understood God was a Spirit, not a man. She had been taught three partners are necessary for a child to be conceived: the mother, the father, and the Holy Spirit. (Ps. 139:16) When God gives His Spirit, life begins. When He withdraws His Spirit, life ends.

Twice before, with the formation of Adam and Eve, God chose to skip the usual birthing process. In this instance, God choose to beget life by His Spirit.

Gabriel answered Mary's question: "The Holy Spirit will come upon you, and the power of the Most High will overshadow you. So, the Holy One to be born of you will be called the Son of God."

When God breaks into a life, He is the truest gentleman. The Lord God Almighty, the Creator of Heaven and Earth, could force submission. It would be His right and privilege. However, it would not be His method.

"I am the Lord's servant," Mary answered him. "May it be to me as you have said."

With her agreement, Mary's world changed in an instant.

And a sign was given to her to let her know she wasn't dreaming.

When Virgins and the Barren Conceive, the Great Physician is On-call

God doesn't mind furnishing proof in the form of witnesses (2 Cor. 13:1), especially in areas that stretch our credulity. In keeping with divine precedent, the angel provided Mary proof that she would conceive and bear the Messiah:

The angel answered, "The Holy Spirit will come upon you, and the power of the Most High will overshadow you. So the holy one to be born will be called the Son of God. Even Elizabeth your relative is going to have a child in her old age, and she who was said to be barren is in her sixth month. For nothing is impossible with God." (Lk. 1:35-37-NIV)

Mary's cousin Elizabeth, the elderly wife of a priest, became a sign, witness, and confidant to the newly pregnant Mary.

Elizabeth also heard Mary's remarkable poetry, which reveals volumes not only about Mary's intelligence and learning, but also her state of mind, hopes, and dreams. From her poem, The Magnificat, we know Mary was so much more than a simple peasant girl. For one so young, she had a keen awareness of inequities, injustice, the pain of others, and a trust that God would eventually make things right.

In it is also hidden Mary's secret.

My soul glorifies the Lord and my spirit rejoices in God my Savior,
For he has been mindful of the humble state of his servant.
From now on all generations will call me blessed,
For the Mighty One has done great things for me – holy is his name.
His mercy extends to those who fear him, from generation to generation.
He has performed mighty deeds with his arm; he has scattered those who are proud in their inmost thoughts.
He has brought down rulers from their thrones but has lifted up the humble.
He has filled the hungry with good things but has sent the rich away empty.
He has helped his servant Israel, remembering to be merciful to Abraham and his descendants forever, even as he said to our fathers. (Lk. 1:47b-51, NIV)

Mary's Other Secret

In the Middle East, when a woman was in labor, friends, family, and neighbors gathered around the house. If the child was a boy, a party broke out. Musicians played and people danced. If the baby was a girl, everyone went away sorrowing. The baby girl would eventually require a dowry when she married and be lost to the clan.

A child's name was significant, too. The name might tell the circumstances surrounding the child's birth, be a blessing for the child, or a curse upon him or her.

Despite fables you may have heard surrounding her birth, in some way, Mary was "a bitterness" to her parents for the name Mary means "bitterness."

Mary echoes the theme of the downtrodden and shortchanged throughout The Magnificat, but never more so in the lines:
My soul glorifies the Lord and my spirit rejoices in God my Savior,
For he has been mindful of the humble state of his servant.
From now on all generations will call me blessed,
For the Mighty One has done great things for me – holy is his name.
"All generations will call me blessed," not bitterness.

Perhaps you think it was a mistake you were ever born. Perhaps, like Mary's parents, you regard life's events as bitter. Remember this: God was there when you were conceived. He knows your name and it isn't Miss Take. He calls you, "Precious Child." He sent His Son, Mary's little boy, to tell you in person.

As the days wore on, the legitimacy of her pregnancy was questioned, and the child's life was threatened. These events Mary treasured in her heart. She could point back to a moment in time when an angel told her she was favored by God and would bear the Christ.

How would she explain this to Joseph? Would she need to?"

Engaged? Espoused? What's the Difference?

Love and romance are Western ideas of what should precede matrimony. In the days of Mary and Joseph, and in some countries today, selecting marriage partners is more like choosing horses for breeding.

Is she from a good family? Is he? What about his reputation? What about his business? Does she have good teeth? A clear complexion? Wide pelvic bones? The list goes on.

Marriage was a business merger between families. Several factors were important:

- ✓ Genetics, because childlessness was tantamount to oblivion
- ✓ Reputation
- ✓ Money

A go-between arranged the marriage between families. Neither bride nor groom was consulted until the two families reached agreement. If either bride or groom objected, the match could be cancelled, but it was a great insult to the rejected party.

Once the agreement was reached and the bride and groom agreed, the groom's family paid a bride price and the bride's family supplied a dowry.

Legally, the couple was married, but they lived apart for a year. The year between the marriage and actual union was the espousal period. In that time the bride assembled what she needed to manage a household. The groom built a new room or suite on his parents' home for his bride.

At the end of the year, with great fanfare, the groom claimed his bride.

Did women get pregnant during the espousal? It happened. It was no crime but considered a trashy embarrassment to both houses. The couple was regarded with suspicion and as morally undisciplined.

What was the effect of Mary's "yes" to God on Joseph's family and carpentry business? Damaging, at the very least. If Mary were stoned to death, it would cleanse their reputation. His family could get a refund on the bride price.

What stopped Joseph? Something more valuable than his reputation and career. Something more precious than gold.

A Man of Compassion

My heart aches as I imagine what went through Joseph's mind and heart at Mary's news:

His surprise and anger went to the depth of his soul. Joseph's flying feet took him past the outskirts of Nazareth into the chalky hills.

I am too trusting. Of all the people who might have betrayed me, I would never have guessed Mary. I thought her to be without guile.

Whenever he thought of the future, he dreamed of Mary. He

considered her soul knit to his own. Now, he questioned if he knew her at all.

Joseph crested the hilltop and slipped into the coolness of a cave. Momentarily blind in the darkness, he closed his eyes to help them adjust.

Exhausted by emotion, Joseph lay on the floor. Mary's face instantly appeared in his mind. The very thought of her made him grind his teeth.

This must be a misunderstanding! his heart cried. But the awful truth remained: Mary was pregnant.

A pregnant espoused wife would hurt business. Who could trust a carpenter who would violate a contract for a few seconds of passion eventually due him anyway? He did not want Mary stoned. It was his right to have his honor avenged and his name cleared.

His imagination saw Mary's eyes wide with fear as the villagers led by rabbis shoved her through the streets to the steep hills surrounding Nazareth. The rabbi read the charge of adultery. Mary turned to quietly face the condemning crowd. Somehow his imagination could not make Mary be guilty. She simply looked at them, never speaking a word. One by one, the jeering crowd fell silent. The rabbis seemed uncertain. They whispered together, and then summoned Joseph to the front. He would be required to throw the first stone.

Someone handed him a large chunk of limestone. His arms held the rock above his head for what seemed like an eternity.

"Stone her! Stone her!"

Mary looked at him, her eyes reaching into his, her mind and soul spoke: "I am not guilty."

He could not throw the rock.

He would divorce her. No matter what anyone else said, no matter what it cost him, he would not take her life.

Despair settled over him. Gradually, he fell into a deep sleep.

For a time, his slumber was heavy and dreamless. Then he felt his mind awaken while his body slept on. He had the sensation of being pulled toward a brilliant light. Joseph panicked but he was powerless to resist. The light was not simply a light, but a person. A voice, laden with authority, commanded him not to fear. To his surprise, he stopped quaking.

"Joseph! Do not be afraid to take Mary as your wife. The child she carries is the Son of the Most High God. Call His name 'Jesus.' He will save His people from their sin."

Joseph was instantly awake.

Climbing out of the cave, he was at peace. He realized those sentences spoken to him by the angel would not only change his life but the future of the whole Jewish race. The long-awaited Messiah was about to be born. He would see the salvation of Israel. He would participate in it.

He knew he needed to make the necessary arrangements for Mary to come to his home. She and the baby needed his protection.

Ninety Miles to Bethlehem

When I stood in Nazareth and looked south toward Bethlehem, I thought, *Ninety miles is a long trot even if you are young and accustomed to walking – especially if you're nine months pregnant.*

I walked a little way in that direction but went the rest of the way by car because I didn't have a week to make the journey on foot. (Okay, that's not the *only* reason I didn't walk the whole ninety miles.)

Historians figure that it only took Mary and Joseph three or four days to walk to Bethlehem. The ancients were tough.

What strikes me remarkable about Mary's journey is this: Although she had a long way to travel, the roughest, rockiest part of her trail was the one that led out of her own hometown.

It's true: It was a steep, scary, downhill climb from Nazareth to the Jezreel Valley before skirting along the Jordan River, then turning toward Bethlehem. Don't kid yourself that going downhill makes it easy. We're talking a steep, check-your-brakes climb down a rocky slope, a one-slip-and-you're-headed-for-breakage drop — especially with her center of gravity hanging low and to the front.

A handmaiden of God must be willing to step out of her comfy circumstances to follow God's leading. Sometimes He forces us to go by sending something unpleasant. In Mary's case, it was a tax increase that forced her out of Nazareth to Bethlehem. How much more unpleasant can you get?

I've thought a lot about the rocky trail of obedience walked by women of faith who — like Mary — say yes to the call of God to serve. They may think they are leaving their home for only a short time, but as Mary found out, God had other things in mind. When she returned years later, she was a very different woman.

A Sword Through the Soul

"No room in the inn," the Scriptures say.

Joseph's family came from Bethlehem, therefore they were related by blood to many families in Bethlehem. And there was a proclivity to marry within your own clan as Abraham and Isaac did. Moreover, hospitality was — and is — a sacred duty. Malachi 3:1-5 warns those who do not care for widows and strangers will be judged by God. Although Mary was "great with Child," yet no one whom Joseph had the right to call on as family sheltered them. Scripture simply says there was no room in the inn. At that time, inns weren't what we think of: big buildings with lots of rooms to let. Or, as some have suggested, an open courtyard within sheltering walls, where people could gather around fires, separate from their animals. The "inn" was a spare room in someone's home. Likely dozens of other relatives got to Bethlehem before them. Scripture says her time had come, so they were probably in a hurry to find shelter. Was Mary's pregnancy a family disgrace? Was she shunned? Again, scripture doesn't say, but when Joseph married her he took responsibility for her. The child to come was considered his.

The owner of the stable where they found shelter did not judge. Scripture doesn't say if he was a relative or an outsider. He saw a young woman who would give birth to her child on the street in full view of everyone if someone didn't help. He offered what he had, likely a little cave hollowed out of the limestone hills. It wasn't much, but if they wanted it...

Here the infant Jesus drew His first breath, and the stable became a holy place.

Two thousand years later, you can visit what many believe was that tiny stable, now in the basement of a mosque and church combination. It is embellished with marble but still holy and unlike any other place on earth.

Although Mary and Joseph's family members and the residents of Bethlehem did not wait outside the stable to burst into song at the words, "It's a boy!" the residents of Jesus' hometown, Heaven, showed up in mass with pyrotechnical glory and assembled an impromptu bash with local shepherds:

An angel of the Lord appeared to them, and the glory of the Lord shone around them, and they were terrified. But the angel said to them, "Do not be afraid. I bring you good news of great joy that will be for all the people. Today in the town of David a Savior has been born to you; he is Christ the Lord. This will be a sign to you: You will find a baby wrapped in cloths and lying in a manger." Suddenly a great company of the heavenly host appeared with the angel, praising God, and saying, "Glory to God in the highest, and on earth peace to men on whom his favor rests." (Lk. 2:9-14)

Bittersweet miraculous moments followed the new family. When Jesus was presented at the temple, two elderly mystics made a beeline to prophesy over the infant (Luke 2). Simeon proclaimed himself ready to die now that he had seen the baby, but chillingly told Mary life would be tough for the child and that "... a sword will pierce your own soul too." (vs. 35b)

Matthew's Gospel tells us that Mary and Joseph remained in Bethlehem after Jesus' birth long enough for Magi to come from the East, possibly Iraq, to worship the babe. Their visit set off an international incident, forcing the young family to flee, and causing a paranoid Herod the Great to slaughter boy babies the age of little Jesus.

News of this horror likely reached Mary and Joseph's ears as they escaped to Egypt. Some of the Bethlehemites whose babies were slaughtered likely would have been friends, acquaintances, or family members.

While the sword spared her child, it indeed pierced her soul.

Because Mother Said So — For a While

The mother-child relationship changes with time and maturity. The Gospels and Acts chronicle two of those relational adjustments between Mary and Jesus.

Consider Jesus in the Temple, making theological pretzels out of the teachers of the Law while worrying His mother and Joseph. Jesus asserted an understanding of His life's purpose and fledging independence with an attitude recognizable by every parent who has endured their teenage child stretching his wings: "Why were you searching for me?" Jesus asked. "Didn't you know I had to be in my Father's house?" (Lk. 2:49-NIV) A generational and spiritual gap existed even then.

But they did not understand what he was saying to them. (Lk. 2:50-NIV)

Yet, (Jesus) went down to Nazareth with them and was obedient to them. (Lk. 2:51, NIV)

Perhaps the story that best characterizes Jesus and Mary's adult pre-ministry relationship is a rather funny one, commonly known as the Marriage at Cana (John 2). This celebration threatened to break up almost before it started due to poor planning on somebody's part — or a tight budget — because they ran out of wine.

Scholars theorize the wedding couple were Mary's relatives because she inserts herself in a situation that otherwise would be none of her business: "Jesus! They have no more wine."

"Dear lady, why are you involving me in this? My time has not yet come," Jesus responds. As the head of Joseph's house, Jesus would be called upon to bless the union and present a gift. But not just yet.

Mary ignored His response. She turned to the servants. "Do whatever He says."

If you are thirty years old and the Son of God, do you have to listen to your mother? I guess so.

So Jesus made water into wine: His first miracle. But don't you wonder what Mary thought He would do?

Once Jesus launched His ministry, He made Capernaum the base of His operations, traveled extensively, and formed a new family from those who followed Him. To underscore this change, as Jesus taught a large crowd, word was passed that His mother and brothers were there to see to Him.

He replied, "My mother and brothers are those who hear God's word

69

and put it into practice." (Lk. 8:21, NIV)

Relationships had changed. His family circle was enlarged to include you and me and the whole world—if we will only hear and do God's word.

Bearing the Truth and Life
Rumors. Lies. Innuendo.

First century people didn't understand Mary or the Son she bore. None of us truly understand them now.

Nazareth townsfolk didn't understand why their village carpenter was suddenly the talk of the Galilee: "Jesus? I knew Him when He was a kid. I know His brothers, sisters, and His mother. They live right over there. Want to see a yoke He made? Makes burdens easy and light."

Once, when Jesus came home to Nazareth for a visit, they nearly stoned Him to death. After that, there is no record of Him ever going back.

As aware of the injustices of the world as the teenage Mary was, it is hard to imagine she'd be clueless as the mother of a grown-up Jesus. The beheading death of her cousin's son, John the Baptist, must have driven her to her knees out of fear for her own Son. The jockeying for power among the disciples, resulting in lobbying by their mother—who from clues found in many places in scripture was also a relative—impacted her, too. There was the growing angry buzz from Jerusalem. She likely heard Jesus predict His own death, something He frequently did.

As mothers, we see our children as they are presently. But our hearts' album preserves snapshots of them as newborns, children, teenagers, babies, toddlers, asleep, taking first steps—all precious moments.

I wonder what Mary's heart saw as she stood at the foot of the cross and watched her Son being tortured to death. As He hung bloody and naked, taking His last breath, did she remember Him as He was on that first Christmas—bloody and naked, taking His first breath?

Did she still see in Him the promise of salvation? Did she still believe His kingdom would never end? Did she still think He was the Son of the Most High?

What did she think when she saw Him risen from the grave, alive forevermore?

One Last Look
The last clear mention of Mary in the scriptures is after Jesus' ascension. She is in the upper room with the rest of Jesus' followers, awaiting the coming of the Holy Spirit. (Acts 1:14.)

There is a possible mention in Romans 16:6. This is no accident: The hand of the Divine wrote this final word on Mary's life.

When we first saw Mary, she was awaiting the promised visitation of the Holy Spirit who would plant the seed of Christ in her womb. When we last see her, she awaits the promised visitation of the Holy Spirit who will plant the seed of Christ in her heart.

Her life and words are shining examples to every soul who desires to be indwelt by the Holy Spirit: "I am the Lord's servant. May it be to me as you have said." (Lk. 2:38a, NIV)

May this be your prayer, too.

Let's Talk About Mary
A. How do you think you would react if your thirteen-year-old daughter made a similar announcement?
B. What is your opinion of ancient writings about Mary that are not included in the canonical Bible? Should they be accepted as truth? Or should the canonical Bible be the sole authority on Mary's life
C. How do you think you would react if you met an angel face-to-face? What questions would you ask the angel if you were asked to carry God's own Son?
D. What clues to Mary's character and personality do you find in The Magnificat?
E. What lines from The Magnificat speak to you?
F. The Holy Spirit that placed the Seed of God in Mary's womb is the same Holy Spirit that places the Seed of God in your heart. As pregnancy changes the shape of a woman, so are our lives changed. What changes have you experienced if you have said, "Be it unto me as you have said"?

Just Between You and God
Has God ever spoken to you about doing something out-of-the-ordinary for Him? What is your response to Him?

Chapter Eight
Anna the Prophetess:
What Was Her Vision for Tomorrow?

In either the rising or setting sun, the limestone walls of old Jerusalem glow — almost pulsate — with golden light. It is as if the blood of the ancients flows through stony capillaries in the limestone. In a way it does, since the hearts of three great religions beat passionately in the Old City.

Old Jerusalem's streets whisper stories from the past. Some tales are familiar; some strange; some defy belief. As you walk the streets, meet the people, and eat the fruit, you begin to see stories as familiar as your name in a new light.

Anna the prophetess's story is that way.

No doubt about it: Anna's passion for Jerusalem ran deep. In her eighty-seven years she saw horrors in its streets that compelled her to answer God's call to the hard life of a prophetess.

What did she see that inspired Anna to fast and intercede day and night for the redemption of Jerusalem? What was she hoping God would do? Were her prayers answered?

Most importantly, why will the prayers of Anna the prophetess change your future — forever?

A Wall of Prayer

Two thousand years ago, the crown jewel of Jerusalem was the temple of God. With its soaring gold-crested sanctuary atop Mount Moriah, contemporary descriptions say that on a clear day, the sheen off the temple could be seen anywhere in Israel.

In 70 AD, Titus destroyed it.

Today, the Dome of the Rock and the Mosque Al-Aqsa occupy the approximate area where the magnificent temple of God once stood. The temple may be gone, but remnants of the retaining wall supporting the foundations still stand. Considered one of the holiest sites in Judaism, the Kotel or the Western Wall is closest to where it is believed the Holy of Holies was located. From all over the world, Jews and Christians come to pray and tuck written prayers between the stones' crevices.

73

Men and women separate to pray as they did in the day when the temple cast its shadow over this place, divided by a curtain but bound across generations by the blood of Abraham and Isaac.

Men tenderly hold small sons or support ancient fathers. With side locks bouncing, they dance and sing with abandon, cry aloud and sway.

But the mood is different on the women's side, more subdued and contemplative. Some shed tears, their prayers offered silently like Hannah's (1 Sam. 1:13). Others reverently touch the wall when they pray, as if reaching for the face of God.

A pregnant young woman, her wildly curly red hair caught in a babushka, says she and her husband left successful careers in the United States to immigrate to Israel when she was expecting their first child.

"Where else can my children live their heritage?" she says as she rests her hand on the bulge that is her second child. "Yes, Israel can be dangerous. But I would rather we all live here and die here than rear my children anywhere else. And there is no place in Israel that I would rather live than Jerusalem. My heart is here, waiting for Messiah."

Another young woman says she is a sabra or a native-born Israeli. She says she is not religious, although she also waits on the Messiah to be revealed. "I don't think Messiah is a person, but the spirit of Israel. Yes, we have enemies who would push us into the sea. But where else can a Jew go besides Israel?"

What petition do they bring to the wall? The peace of Jerusalem, they both say. And that Messiah will come soon and bring that peace.

Two thousand years ago, very near this very spot where women still come to pray for the coming of the Messiah, the prophetess Anna prayed the same prayer. When she saw Baby Jesus, she declared her prayers to be answered. But were they? If so, why do Jewish women still pray for the Messiah to come?

Why is Anna called a prophetess? What did she see? Were her prayers answered on Palm Sunday? Or Easter? Or does the spirit of Anna still look forward to another redemption of Jerusalem?

The answers may surprise you.

A Dawning

Imagine with me how life was for Anna, worshipping constantly in the temple ...

Sometimes in the chilly early morning hours, Anna still missed the arms of her long-dead husband. Although they were married for only seven years, remaining single was her choice, difficult though it was. Her life's work was too demanding to accommodate a man and marriage.

Born to the house of Asher, its territory along the coast, the sea called to her. But her heart was in the temple of God — her true home. At eighty-seven, she never left the temple. Aware her time on earth was growing short, she was also aware her life's purpose was to pray, "Send the Redeemer, O Lord!"

It was a race to the finish between her and Simeon. He also had some years on him, but he also had something Anna did not: an assurance that he would not die until the Messiah came.

Please, Lord, please let me see the Redeemer of Jerusalem! Then I will die happy and fulfilled, was her constant prayer.

Anna lay in the darkness, eyes closed, listening, her soul inquiring, her bones protesting supporting her for another day. Prolonged fasting left her body weak while sharpening her mind and spirit with crystal alertness.

Please speak to me, Lord. Your maidservant is listening.

Promises from Scriptures flittered through her refreshed mind:

"You, Bethlehem, are small among the clans but out of you will come One who will rule over Israel, whose origins are from ancient times." (Mic. 5:2, paraphrase)

As Anna contemplated this prophecy, it stirred recollections of Israel's glory days under David's rule. Was the Spirit reminding her that from the line of the Bethlehem-born shepherd king the Messiah would come?

From Bethlehem, O Lord? The Messiah will be another shepherd king?

The words of Isaiah came to her mind: To us a son is born, and the government will be on his shoulders. He will be called Wonderful Counselor, Mighty God, Everlasting Father, Prince of Peace. His government will increase, and peace will be unending. He will reign on David's throne, establishing and upholding it with justice and righteousness from forever. (Is, 9:6,7, paraphrase)

Anna saw signs God was about to do something new:

In the past year, an elderly priest, Zechariah, saw an angel in the Holy of Holies. Anna was in the crowd of worshippers who waited and waited for Zechariah's blessing (Luke 1), only to see him making signs that he had seen an angel. Then later, Zechariah and his wife experienced another miracle when a baby was born to them in their old age; a child prophesied to be the forerunner of the Messiah.

Scholars were teaching that the Messiah would be born seventy-seven generations from Creation—dates perfectly coordinating with Daniel's prophecies regarding the coming of the Messiah (Dan. 7:24).

Then, a little over a month ago, a strange report issued from Bethlehem. Shepherds told of a visitation of angels proclaiming a baby in a manger was a Savior and Christ the Lord.

A fresh revelation blew through Anna's spirit like wind rising before dawn. Age may have dimmed Anna's eyesight, but she clearly saw it was a new day for Jerusalem. The city of God would glow with holiness like a bride on her wedding day. The time was now. Creation's calendar was reset. The Messiah was born!

However, this was news that could get her killed by King Herod's secret police. What did God want her to do with it?

Lord God, do I keep these glad tidings quiet? Or do I tell everyone?

Secrets to Fasting and Prayer

(Anna) never left the temple but worshiped night and day, fasting and praying... (Lk. 2:37b, NIV)

Diets...don't you hate them? Some diets — or spiritual fasts — are more beneficial to our souls than to our bodies, which is very probably why they are so hard to follow.

We see in scripture God expects us to fast. Jesus said, "When you fast..." not "If you fast..." He also gave a tutorial on how to conduct your private times of prayer and fasting. (Mt. 6:5-18)

Fasting for spiritual reasons can be harder than dieting. Satan knows fasting is a powerful weapon against him. Expect him to use a ruse similar to one successful with Eve in the garden by questioning whether fasting is actually "God's will." Then he will target your senses with your favorite goodies. (Mt. 17:21)

God honors the person who denies her own fleshly desires to devote herself to prayer and fasting, just as He did Anna.

While we don't know exactly what kind of fast Anna followed, let's look at a few of the famous diets — or fasts — in the Bible: (my labels)

Adam and Eve Fast (Genesis 2 and 3)

Perfect world, perfect man, perfect woman, perfect communication with God — everything was perfect — yet they were still on a diet! To teach them a multitude of lessons, they were to refrain from eating the fruit of one tree. They didn't.

An Adam and Eve Fast is giving up one craved item of food — perhaps chocolate — for closer communion with God. This is similar to giving up something for Lent, but it may be practiced any time of year.

Manna Fast (Exodus 16)

In the wilderness, the Israelites were sent manna (literally translated: "What is it?") or a heaven-sent bread. With it, the Lord demonstrated rewards reaped by following His simple rules for gathering manna. Contrast that against facing a breakfast of stinking worms when they disobeyed them. This was an important lesson to learn if they were to conquer the Promised Land. The Israelites griped a lot about the manna. They had a taste for something meaty with garlic and onions (Nm. 11:5).

A Manna Fast is giving up all foods except one—perhaps brown rice—to hear direction for your future and find courage to follow the Lord's leading.

Kosher Fast (Leviticus 11)

There are many regulations associated with a kosher diet, much of which deals with clean and unclean animals, food combinations, and how animals are slaughtered. God said He prescribed the kosher diet to set the Jews apart "to be holy because I am holy." (vs. 44)

A Kosher Fast is one way to demonstrate that an individual is set apart and belongs to God.

Daniel Fast (Daniel 1)

When Daniel and his three friends became captives in Babylon, they chose a vegetarian diet rather than eat unclean meats. God gave all four of these young men knowledge and understanding. Daniel, however, was especially gifted with the ability to understand visions and dreams.

A Daniel Fast is for those who crave skill and wisdom.

A Total Fast (Mt. 4:2)

Before embarking on His ministry, Jesus went without food for forty days and forty nights. The Bible specifies that His fast was day and night to differentiate from those in Middle Eastern culture who fast during the day but feast at night.

A Total Fast is one way to seek God's face and power for ministry service.

This is by no means a comprehensive list of biblical fasts, but this should—dare I say it?—whet your appetite for more information.

Before you fast, check with your doctor. By all means check with God for His approval. Remember: You are not fasting to lose weight but to increase your hunger for God.

During the fast, drink plenty of water, refrain from sexual relations (1 Cor. 7:5), keep your fast private (Mt. 6:18), and get rest.

But why—or what—would drive a person to choose a life of prayer and fasting? Why was the redemption of Jerusalem more important to Anna than marriage and children—or food? And what did Anna know that you need to know?

A Temple in Need of Cleansing

Consider the setting for this historic moment through Anna's eyes:

Her gaze swept up to the high ramparts of the Antonia Fortress where Herod garrisoned some 600 soldiers. Sunshine gleamed off helmets and spear tips as soldiers watched from the rooftop.

Located on the north side of the temple complex in Jerusalem's most vulnerable spot, the Antonia was supposed to be for the city's protection. It served a dual purpose: it protected Herod from the people while keeping an eye on worshippers. Nothing—not even the temple—was sacred from prying eyes.

Now that Anna was certain the Messiah was born, she knew she had to be vigilant. Herod had spies everywhere. He was so dangerously paranoid that he slaughtered his own sons rather than let either of them become king. If Herod caught the slightest hint that a new king of the Jews was born...

Please protect Your Anointed One from the hand of Herod.

Anna clearly remembered the years before Herod ruled: the days of her youth when Jewish kings, called the Hasmoneans, ruled Judea rather than a Roman lackey like Herod. When the Roman senate declared Herod "King of the Jews," Anna thought "Murderer of the Jews" was a far more accurate title. Herod wasn't their true king. Nor could he ever be

She remembered Herod riding into Jerusalem on a white horse to claim the crown and throne. So many Jews died in the uprising, blood literally ran in the streets. Herod barely had anyone left to rule. Piles of corpses. The smell of the dead. Babies crying with hunger.

Thank You, Lord, that the Messiah will rule with justice and mercy.

Herod's incessant building sparked new wealth, but Anna saw how his influence was bringing moral poverty. Beginning with the king and his court, immorality was rampant. Jerusalem's young were forsaking the LORD God for Greek gods and culture. Few religious leaders had the courage—or moral authority—to speak against it. Some, like the Sadducees who now controlled the temple and supported the Romans, had sold their souls and their God for money and power.

Forgive us, Lord. Please do not judge us according to our deeds but according to Your great faithfulness, mercy, and love.

The cloud of sin that hung over Jerusalem was enough to discourage the most optimistic. Anna wasn't an optimist: She was a believer in the Word of God. God promised the Messiah and a new golden age of peace, prosperity, justice, and righteousness. Anna stubbornly clung to that promise.

May the Redeemer turn hearts to You.

She dreamed of a New Jerusalem, beautiful like a bride on her wedding day. Into the open gates of the New Jerusalem the Messiah would ride on a white horse, all enemies defeated.

Anna's bones protested as she walked the stone promenade to the southern Huldah Gates. Tradition said that Huldah, the prophetess of old, sat here when delivering her prophecies (2 Kings 22:14). Since most worshippers entered the Temple complex through the southern gates main entrance, and they faced Bethlehem, this would be the place she would wait for Him to appear.

Lord, please let me recognize Him. Please don't let me miss Him.

Temple Rituals for Parents and Baby

On the eighth day, when it was time to circumcise Him, He was named Jesus, the name the angel had given Him before He had been conceived. When the time of their purification according to the Law of Moses had been completed, Joseph and Mary took Him to Jerusalem to present Him to the Lord (as it is written in the Law of the Lord, "Every firstborn male is to be consecrated to the Lord," and to offer a sacrifice in keeping with what is said in the Law of the Lord: a pair of doves or two young pigeons.)." (Lk. 2:21-23, NIV)

Three Jewish rituals are described in the above passage:

Circumcision and naming ceremony. This sacred event took place when Jesus was eight days old but was not necessarily done in the temple.

Presentation of a redemption fee for the firstborn (Nm. 18:16). This was to be paid to the priests a little over a month after the child's birth.

The sacrifice for the mother's purification after childbirth (Lev. 12:8). A lamb and pigeon were to be sacrificed at the temple forty days after a boy was born. If the parents were poor, two pigeons could be substituted. A financially strapped Mary and Joseph brought two pigeons.

These last two ceremonies were the items of worship that brought together Joseph, Mary, Jesus, and Anna for one shining moment. And what the prophetess saw in the innocent face of Jesus changes the future for us all.

Anna's Emancipation Proclamation

A man, hard-muscled and weather-beaten, held a small cage containing two pigeons. The woman, so young she was almost a child herself, cradled a tiny child. Although Anna couldn't see the baby for His wrappings, she knew. The Spirit stirred in Anna's soul the moment she spotted them coming through the gate. *The Baby! He's the One! O Lord, You have sent the Redeemer of Jerusalem!*

The Spirit urged her to follow them.

Although she knew the couple had come to the Temple to worship, Anna had to see the baby's face. She struggled to her feet to follow.

Please, Lord. May I be so privileged as to look on the face of the Messiah?

Suddenly, a crowd of enthusiastic pilgrims swept through the gates, nearly toppling her to the pavement. Two men caught her. "Sorry, grandmother," one said and helped steady her.

Anna regained her footing and frantically scanned the vast outer

Court of the Gentiles. Vanished! The young couple and their baby were gone!

Open my eyes. Lord, help me to find them! Please, oh please, don't let me miss the moment of Your visitation!

The altar! She knew the couple would be taking their pigeons to the place of sacrifice. Fighting the crowds, Anna pushed her way forward, painstakingly climbing the stairs, to the entrance of the Court of the Women. Then the Spirit moved upon her soul again. She stopped.

Shall I wait here, Lord?

The couple and their baby were nowhere to be seen. She glanced around impatiently. There were other entrances and exits. She might miss them entirely.

How long shall I wait, Lord?

Her question was answered almost immediately. A few yards away, almost behind her, she saw the couple. Simeon was with them. He took the baby in his arms, his wrinkled face wreathed in joy. Studying the baby for a long minute, he looked skyward. The sun's reflection on the temple's golden crest bathed his features in radiance.

"Sovereign Lord, now dismiss Your servant in peace. My eyes have seen a light for revelation to the Gentiles and for glory to Your people— Your Salvation."

A look of amazement passed between the man and woman as if the secret they shared was spoken aloud.

But Simeon was not yet finished. He laid his gnarled hand on the shoulder of the man. "The Lord bless you, Joseph."

Then Simeon moved his hand to the woman's head, his expression transformed by sudden sorrow. "This child of yours will cause many people in Israel to collapse and others to rise up. He will be a warning sign. Many people will reject Him. And you, Mary, will suffer like you have been stabbed with a dagger."

At these ominous words, Mary reached for her child as if to protect Him from the future. Joseph drew her close to his side.

Now, Lord?

Anna stepped forward. "Thank You, Almighty God, for this child, the Redeemer of Jerusalem!"

Stunned, Simeon, Mary, and Joseph looked at her.

Anna smiled at their surprise. "May I see the Redeemer?"

Mary nodded. Pulling back His wrappings, Anna looked upon the face of God.

Eyes That See a Bright Tomorrow

The Scriptures say Anna "spoke about the Child to all who were looking forward to the redemption of Jerusalem." (Lk. 2:38, NIV) From that moment on, Anna's purpose in life was to spread the hope birthed by the coming of Jesus.

Some will ask, "How is Jesus the Redeemer of Jerusalem? That city is still in turmoil."

Good question. Through His death and resurrection, Jesus redeems ruined lives. But He was not then, nor do the Jews now, recognize Him as their Messiah. Yet one day, on bended knee, the whole world will recognize Him as the Redeemer and a New Jerusalem will open her gates (Rev. 21:2-4).

It's true: Evil has made great inroads. It can cause some to be so discouraged that they don't even want to bring children into the world.

But a great blessing comes to women of any age who, like Anna, devote themselves to fasting and prayer. To them, like Anna, God gives a vision of what their countries, towns, churches, and homes can become. He shows them the happy end of the story when He wipes away every tear, when death, mourning, crying, and pain are abolished, and then the lion and lamb lie down together, and Jesus makes everything new (Is. 11:6, Rev. 21:4, 5).

Anna saw the problems. However, she didn't gossip or gripe. Instead, she fasted and prayed that God's kingdom would come; His will would be done in her hometown and the Temple as it was in heaven (Lk. 11:2). Anna the prophetess teaches women everywhere to push evil out of their communities on their knees.

Let's Talk About Anna
A. Many people see the future as bleak. How do you see the future? Rosy? Dark? Why?
B. What good things would you like to see the future bring to your children and grandchildren?
C. What good things could you be praying that the future will bring? How could your prayers be turned into actions on your part?
D. Have you ever fasted? Why do you think God calls people to fast? Why is self-discipline important for someone who loves God?
E. When Anna and Simeon saw the Baby Jesus, they believed that although Israel was under Rome, their people had a future. According to their words, what do you think they expected the Messiah to do?
F. If you could ask God for a blessing for the future of your family, town, state, and country, what would it be?

Chapter Nine
The Woman at the Well:
Why Did Jesus Go Out of His Way to Ask Her for a Drink?

Craving. Yearning constantly.

The Samaritan woman at the well had an itch she could not scratch, a pain she could not alleviate, a thirst that would not be quenched.

She tried. Over and over.

Some women try to satisfy that longing with food. Or shopping. Or power. Or beauty. Or_____? (Fill in the blank.)

Many women, like the woman at the well, think the deep cry of their souls can be satisfied with romance and sex and a man, a soulmate, a lover.

The fantasy of meeting Prince Charming and living happily ever after seems to be engrained in the hearts of women. Some ceaselessly seek the prince whose kiss can break the evil spell. There is such a prince. But His name is not Charming.

The woman at the well met Him — but not in her damaging fantasies. Finally.

You can meet Him, too.

We don't know her name, but we'll call the Samaritan woman at the well Umnia, which means "longing" or "desire" in Arabic, for she longed for love and acceptance — something as basic to survival as the water she drew from the well.

In the strictly cultural context of the day, the entire story of Umnia is so incredible as to be almost unbelievable. In those days, men did not publicly speak to women: Jews did not associate with Samaritans. In fact, Jews went miles out of the way to avoid Samara. Eating anything from a Samaritan's hand — much less directly asking for food or drink from a Samaritan woman — was tantamount to eating from the dog's dish or drinking from the toilet.

In addition to that, Umnia was guilty — guilty of repeated failure, immorality, and only God knew what else. Her own village despised her.

But the Apostle John, who records Umnia's story in his gospel, said Jesus deliberately went through Samaria. (Jn. 4:4) Did Jesus intentionally seek her? Did Jesus know something about Umnia that made Him defy all traditions for a rendezvous with her?

What does their meeting mean for those whose lives are characterized by failure? To those driven by guilt?

And what offer does Jesus, Prince of Peace, extend to you that He first offered to the woman at the well? (Hint: It is the one thing you have always desired in life.)

Water, Water, Not Everywhere

Roses. Tomatoes. Grapes. Jojoba trees. Lush vineyards, orchards, and gardens. Does this sound like a description of the Garden of Eden?

Surprise! They all grow in the barren Negev Desert.

Plants and trees appear to be growing by some miracle since yearly rainfall in the Negev is anywhere between a scant inch and half a foot.

The Negev (derived from the Latin meaning "deserted" or "abandoned" or in Hebrew "dry") has the wild beauty and wasted promise of a rebellious child. The ground is fertile, the area vast, but without rain, it is fruitless.

Yet vegetation thrives, not by divine miracle, but because of the clever technology of advanced irrigation methods.

The Negev surface looks like a moonscape with plants growing by magic. However, a look under the surface reveals tiny spigots planted at the root tips acting as fountains of life to each individual plant. Recycled from city sewers, the water travels miles and miles through a complicated, state-of-the-art system to thirsty roots.

"Recycling water like this is poetry," the irrigation manager said, when I spoke with him on my visit that day. "Think of it: Sewer water produces beautiful flowers, wine, and skin care lotions."

Long ago, it took backbreaking effort — largely provided by women — to conserve and provide water for thirsty plants and people. Israel has two seasons each year, wet and dry. Rain must be collected during the wet season, then conserved during the dry.

The ancients employed a crude but clever technology to accomplish this. Most homes had a cistern, or a clay-lined underground tank, into which runoff rainwater was collected and stored. This water was drawn for household chores. In a drought emergency, when wells went dry, stagnant, bacteria-laden cistern water might need to be drunk for survival. As you can imagine, cistern water could be muddy, unhealthy, and flavored by spiders and bugs.

Much preferred is "living water" from underground springs. Purified by percolating through layers of sand, living water is clean, life-sustaining, and refreshing. The deeper the well, the better the water.

Collecting living water was an arduous job assigned to women.

Narrow stone steps needed to be chiseled through yards of limestone to reach the mouth of the well. After that, a jug and rope were required to haul the water to the surface. Once filled, the heavy jug would be carried up the steps, now slippery with water and without handrails — not handicapped accessible or user friendly for pregnant women!

At first light, women trudged to the well to collect the day's supply of water. Standing on the steps, waiting their turn to draw water, they exchanged news, gossip, and friendship with kindred spirits.

But there is another source of living water found in the most unlikely place: the desert. Artesian wells crisscross underground throughout the Negev. A sharp stick poked into the ground in just the right spot brings fresh water shooting to the surface, producing a fountain of living water that springs up.

To find living water fountains takes incredible luck. Or someone who recognizes the signs and can point to the spot and say, "Trust me. There's water here. Ask me for living water and I'll give you a fountain of life."

But if, like Umnia, you've been misled so many times, how — or whom — can you trust that you will not be left thirsty in the desert?

Droplets of Truth

Imagine with me that landmark day ...

Umnia squinted at the sky. Noon. The merciless sun had driven nearly everyone else into shelter.

It's safe now, she thought.

Shouldering her water jug and rope, she trudged down the limestone steps into the dim cave covering the village well.

Out of the darkness came a man's voice: "Will you give Me a drink of water?"

She blinked.

Something felt familiar here.

Then she knew. It was a line from the age-old romance between Isaac and Rebekah. Abraham's servant asked Rebekah, the maiden of Nahor and Umnia's ancestor, the same question: "Will you give me a drink of water?" And Rebekah found the love of her life — someone Umnia fruitlessly searched for.

She didn't think she could bear any more pain. Her life was all pain. Even the simple, daily act of drawing water was filled with pain and loneliness.

"Whore!" the village women hissed as she passed them. She had known them all her life, but they held her in contempt, whispering behind their hands, shoving sharp elbows in her ribs, spitting in her face, slyly tripping her on the steps — all told her she wasn't welcome. To avoid them, she came to the well in the heat of the noonday.

The man watched from the shadows. Stray sunbeams played over His features and from the tassels on His clothes and other cultural distinctions, Umnia could see He was a Jew.

"Please," He said. "A drink."

For hundreds of years, a religious argument caused the Jews to hold the Samaritans in contempt. Yet this Man — obviously a Jew — was asking for a drink. He had to be taunting her. Why?

"You are a Jew, and I am a Samaritan. Yet You ask me for a drink?"

"If you knew the gift of God and Who is asking you for a drink, you would have asked Him and He would have given you living water."

She was confused. "Sir, the well is deep and You have no jug or rope with which to draw. Where — and how — can You get this living water?"

He sat silent and waiting.

She snorted cynically. "Are You greater than our father Jacob, who gave us the well and drank from it himself, as did also his sons and his flocks and herds?"

The man countered, "Everyone who drinks Jacob's well water will be thirsty again. But whoever drinks the water I give will never thirst. The water I give becomes a spring of water welling up to eternal life."

She contemplated this. He seemed sincere, but she had been fooled by the promises of men before. Somehow His promises seemed impossible, but her soul was drawn to Him.

Liar! Umnia's memories screamed. *Men are all liars! Let Him just try to keep this promise.*

"All right, sir. Give me this water so that I won't get thirsty and keep coming here to draw water."

"Go get your husband and come back."

Caught! She didn't want to tell Him the truth; strangely, she couldn't lie to Him. But she didn't want to recount the sordid details of her life. If He knew her — really knew her — would He say she was a waste of living water? Would He see that her soul was like a cistern filled with the mud of life's runoff?

"I have no husband," she replied.

"You're right when you say you have no husband. The fact is you've had five husbands. The man you now live with is not your husband. What you said is quite true."

She was stunned. *How did He know? What else does He know about my life?*

And would He still give her this miraculous living water?

Fountains of Fantasy

Did you ever want something — or someone — so much you thought you couldn't live if you were denied? Then when you got it, did it disappoint you? The sad truth is this: things in life are not always what they appear.

In the desert, mirages are common. The hotter the day, the more mirages appear. The thirstier you are, the more fevered fantasies insist the mirages are real.

Mirages are refracted light or mirrored images of the sky. They can, in fact, be photographed.

But mirages are not water. They never satisfy thirst.

Mirages of life — food, romance, sex, food, drugs, alcohol, shopping, success, fame, beauty — shimmer enticingly like an oasis in the desert. Try to drink from them and you will choke on dry sand.

Solomon found this out with his great experiment with life. Because he had unlimited resources, he denied himself nothing his heart desired — wealth, love and sex — he had 700 wives and 300 concubines! — education, wisdom, and more.

He summarized his experiment as "Vanity! Vanity! All is vanity!" (Ecc. 1:2, paraphrase) In modern vernacular: "You're only kidding yourself if you think those things will make you happy! I repeat: you're only kidding yourself if you think those things will make you happy!"

He advises, "Remember your Creator while you are young." (Ecc. 12:1, paraphrase) Restated for clarity: "Don't waste your youth chasing mirages. Seek God, the Source of life."

Having reached the pinnacle of success in the ancient world, the psalmist and king, David penned this: "As the deer pants for streams of water, my soul pants for You, O God. My soul thirsts for the living God. When can I meet with Him?" (Ps. 42:1-2, paraphrase)

But what if you're like Umnia and have chased mirage after mirage? What if life's runoff has left you polluted? Can you ever be clean again and filled with thirst-quenching Living Water?

Worship at the Well

Umnia was thunderstruck. He knew about her five husbands. How?

Having had five divorces, she didn't bother with formalities. She simply lived with her lovers. Her promises — and theirs — proved worthless.

What else does He know about me?

"You are a prophet!" she exclaimed. "Answer a question for me: Our fathers worshiped on this mountain, but you Jews claim the place to worship is in Jerusalem. What do You think?"

"Believe me, the time is coming when you will not worship the Father either on this mountain nor in Jerusalem. The time is here now when true worshipers will reverence the Father in spirit and truth. This is the kind of worshipers the Father seeks. God is spirit, and His worshipers must worship in spirit and truth."

Umnia contemplated His strange words. Was this true? Did God care less about rituals or where people worshipped but desired genuine love for Him?

These were new, troubling ideas. If what the stranger said was true, sacrificing animals didn't erase her sins. God wanted her to live hand-in-hand with Him.

She wasn't certain she could. What about the destruction left in the wake of her bad choices? She needed help beyond herself. It would take a miracle for her to change.

"I know that the Messiah is coming. When He comes, He will explain everything to us," she hedged.

The Man declared, "I am the Messiah."

Umnia stared at the Man.

This Man is the Messiah? In Samaria? Talking to me? Is He the One prophesied to set the captives free? Will He still give me Living Water that satisfies my thirsty soul?

Umnia heard footfalls on the stairway and turned to face a crowd of men. Who were they and what did they want?

The Headwaters of Life

"...true worshipers will worship the Father in spirit and truth. This is the kind of worship the Father seeks..."

Keeping rules and laws didn't bring peace or satisfaction.

The blood of animals didn't repair destroyed lives.

What does God want from us? How do we worship God in "spirit and in truth"? And what is "Living Water"?

No more riddles. It's time to be plain.

The human soul in its most basic state is lonely. It longs. It yearns. It thirsts.

At first, a newborn is satisfied with her mother's milk. Soon she becomes an intrepid explorer. Her searching continues until she finds her place in the grand scheme of life.

All search. Some find their place: some do not.

Jesus' claim is this: "I am What you are looking for. I am Who you are looking for. 'I am the Way, the Truth, and the Life. No one comes to the Father except through Me.'" (Jn. 14:6, NIV)

Your place is as a beloved child of God. No matter who you are or what you've done, Jesus came to bring you to the Father. With Him your soul will be satisfied.

He wants you. Come as you are. No lies or pretense from you. No lies or pretense from Him. Your spirit can communicate honestly and openly with His. His Spirit will guide you through any deserts you must pass through. He'll tell you if you are seeing a mirage or an oasis.

No cistern water for you! He will lead you away from stagnant waters, not to them. (Ps. 23:3) The Fountain of Life will refresh your soul. You will flourish like a tree planted by a river! (Psalm 1)

Spring Cleaning
In the narrative of the woman at the well, John's gospel gently pokes fun at how he and the other disciples were so flabbergasted to see Jesus chatting with a woman that they couldn't bring themselves to question "Why?"

Umnia left her water jar at the well and invited the town to meet Jesus, "the Man who told me everything I ever did."

You can almost hear the townsfolk murmur, "What a sordid tale that must have been!" Out of curiosity, they came to hear Jesus and invited Him to stay and teach, and He did for two days.

Umnia's openness about her past failures brought people to Jesus: His own words convinced them that He was the Messiah, the Savior of the world, and the Living Water.

Jesus came for the lowly, the failure, the immoral, the wasted, for everyone. Be warned: If you come to Him, He won't allow you to stay as you are. He will do for you what He did for the woman at the well: He'll refresh your soul.

Let's Talk About the Woman at the Well
A. Women semi-seriously joke about "loving chocolate." Why do you think many women turn to chocolate or another type of food for happiness or comfort?
B. What do you observe women doing to alleviate stress, sadness, disappointment, rejection, boredom, etc.?
C. What do you think women who have multiple intimate relationships are searching for?
D. Because of her immoral behavior, her community shunned Umnia. How should we treat people whose lifestyles we disapprove of?
E. Do you think Jesus went out of His way to talk to Umnia? Why or why not?
F. Although Umnia had a checkered past, why do you think her past was not an obstacle to Jesus?
G. What do you think Jesus was offering Umnia? What does the term "living water" mean to you?

Just Between You and God
What yearnings does God wish to satisfy in you?

Chapter Ten
Dorcas:
She Built a Church with a Needle

Would you like to do something for Jesus that would continue for 2,000 years?

Dorcas did, although she probably didn't know it would. That's often the way it is with the simplest acts of human kindness. Done in Jesus' name, they can change the world.

As if to maximize the impact of her life, Dorcas' story is told in only a few short verses, exploding from the pages of the Bible with bombshell after bombshell.

She is known by two names: Dorcas and Tabitha. Typically, someone who has a dual identity, an alias, or a stage name has something to hide, but that isn't the case here. Both names mean the same thing in two different languages: "gazelle."

Quite often, people in the Bible had several names, either because of being discussed in several languages, or because their names changed due to life events, such as Simon's name being changed to Peter, or Saul's name being changed to Paul. In Dorcas's case, she dealt with people from several cultures/languages, so both her names were given.

The text unabashedly states a fact that prompts yet another question: What role did Dorcas play in Jesus' ministry? The scripture says Dorcas/Tabitha was a "disciple." (Acts 9:36) Some with a certain theological skew might challenge this as a sort of politically correct translation, but the Scriptures are clear: Dorcas/Tabitha was, in fact, a "disciple."

So what do female disciples do? Is their role any different than the male disciples? We hear a lot about the twelve disciples who were closest to Jesus, but they weren't the only disciples He had. Jesus certainly did have female followers who played a vital part in His ministry. The way they—and Dorcas—furthered His ministry provides valuable patterns for women today searching for meaningful, fulfilling ways to express their love for Jesus.

And that leads us to the life and amazing ministry of Dorcas/Tabitha and perhaps the biggest bombshell: While many disciples met with untimely deaths in her day, what was it about Dorcas/Tabitha and her ministry that was so important that God brought her back to life?

And the question that goes with it: What happened to the church that Dorcas/Tabitha built—with a needle? That's right: Dorcas/Tabitha built a church with a needle!

To find the answers to these questions, come with me to the ancient seaport city of Jaffa (or Joppa) where we will search the Scriptures. Here we find yet another surprise: Dorcas/Tabitha still lives!

A Stitch in Time

Jaffa (also known as "Joppa" or "Yafa") should be on every tourist's agenda. As I discovered on my visit, the sun-dappled streets are an adventure for the eye as well as a shopper's delight. Intriguing vistas invite exploration while breezes off the sea cool luminous serpentine walkways where artistic wares are displayed at every hand.

Ancient Jaffa lays cheek-to-jowl with modern Tel Aviv, but in large part, it has been replaced by the newer city in commercial importance. Long ago, however, Jaffa's natural harbor was a shipping hub and figured prominently in many Bible stories:

It was from Jaffa that the reluctant prophet Jonah determinedly sailed away from his preaching assignment in Nineveh.

In Jaffa, while awaiting a call to dinner at the seaside house of Simon the tanner, a tablecloth from heaven was let down before a hungry Simon Peter. A familiar Voice issued the invitation to eat from this amazing banquet of "unclean animals" three times before Peter realized that it really was Jesus speaking and He was serious. At that same time and place, Peter received the shattering revelation that Jesus was calling Gentiles to faith in Him and forgiveness, not just Jews.

It was also in Jaffa that a woman—Dorcas/Tabitha—built a church with a needle. (Be patient: the proof of this statement will appear in due time.) That church still survives and thrives, and amazingly, so does the generous spirit of Dorcas.

By looking carefully at what we can discover from the text, the time, and the town, an amazing portrait of Dorcas/Tabitha emerges. This ancient needlewoman is sending you and me an eternal pattern for weaving significance. With her seams, Dorcas/Tabitha shares the 2,000-year-old secret for living a meaningful life.

The Ancient Secret Code of Women

Long before women in the Underground Railroad sewed symbols into their quilts that served as a code for travelers to help them find safe shelter, daughters of the desert wove a clandestine language into their needlework. The colorful, intricate designs with which they adorned clothing are a secret code.

This code, passed down from generation to generation among the Bedouins, is still in use today, as I learned on one of my visits to Israel. The intricate needle patterns and colors on women's clothing advertise her biography in intimate detail. For example: blue triangles sewn into the hem of a woman's dress advertise she is a virgin. Red triangles, representing drops of blood, say the opposite.

That is just the beginning. Life stories may be stitched onto purses or bodices. Entire tribal histories may be traced on a saddle blanket or other personal item. But to read the story, you must know the code.

Needlework can tell much more than that. It can tell the profound story of a love that changes lives, as it did with Dorcas/Tabitha. Let's follow the thread of her story...

The Severed Silver Cord

In Joppa there was a disciple named Tabitha (which, when translated, is Dorcas), who was always doing good and helping the poor. About that time, she became sick and died, and her body was washed and placed in an upstairs room... (Acts 9:36-37, NIV)

Imagine the scene with me:

Flickering shadows danced upon the stony chamber walls as stricken mourners approached her body, then blanched in horror. Surely this corpse was not their beloved Dorcas! Everyone described her as the most beautiful woman they ever knew. But as she lay dead, she was unrecognizable. All the familiar landmarks of her face were missing — her sweet smile, the laugh lines at the corners of her eyes, her dimple.

Only her clothing and hands looked familiar. A woolen outer robe lay folded beside her body. She was simply dressed in a well-cut linen shift with classic, white-on-white adornment. No one remembered seeing her wearing anything else. Of all the garments she made for others, after her death it was discovered her shift was all the clothing she personally owned.

Her long, supple fingers crossed over her breast displayed dressmaker calluses earned by working on her loom and plying her needle.

Mourners huddled together tearfully, casting quick, furtive glances at her body. Suddenly, they felt naked again. How would they ever survive in a world without Dorcas?

As word spread throughout the city of Jaffa, the upper chamber grew crowded with the sorrowing. Dorcas' friends were varied, divided, and multilingual. The Greeks called her "Dorcas." Those who spoke Aramaic, a Hebrew dialect, called her "Tabitha." Some in the garment trade knew

Dorcas only professionally. There was her church family. Simon, the tanner, for instance, knew Dorcas both as a fellow tradesperson and as a sister in Christ.

Most conspicuous were the widows and little children. "Dorcas made this for me," they said to each other, displaying sturdy, serviceable garments sewn from quality remnants.

Dorcas' colleagues and clients viewed the tearful displays from the poor with disgust. They knew that Dorcas was a disciple of Jesus, but they were horrified to learn she squandered her talent upon such a motley herd of undesirables. Likely, they hinted broadly to one another, she contracted her fatal illness from one of them.

The crowds surrounding Dorcas's house parted as a tall, burly man with a crisply curling beard came into the house. Head bowed, he seemed to be praying as he approached the bier where her body lay.

An elderly widow touched his elbow. "See this, Peter? Dorcas made these for me." Her voice quavered with emotion as she held out her shift and robe for his inspection. "When I was naked, she clothed me."

A young woman, holding the hand of a small child and balancing a baby upon her hip, stepped forward. "My husband was lost at sea, but she made clothing for my whole family."

One after another, the poorest of the poor bore testimony to Dorcas's largess and love.

"Please leave," Peter murmured softly. "All of you."

The mourners looked at each other questioningly. What was Peter going to do?

Just What Did Women Disciples Do?

"Thank You, God, that I was not born a Gentile, a woman, or a slave."

This was the daily prayer Jewish women heard their fathers, husbands, brothers, or sons pray. (*Tosefta* to Berakhlot 6:16)

While Jesus' miracles and teaching rattled the religious in the Galilee region, His private act of compassion toward a woman with a checkered past (Luke 7) drew women from all over the district to His side. Prior to His merciful words, "Your sins are forgiven. Go in peace," most women lived in terror of a vengeful God. But if Jesus could assure a repentant woman, well known for her moral slip-ups, of forgiveness, there was at last hope.

... Jesus traveled about from one town and village to another, proclaiming the good news of the kingdom of God. The Twelve were with him, and also some women who had been cured of evil spirits and diseases ... and many others. These women were helping to support them out of their own means. (Lk. 8:1-3, NIV)

Women loved Jesus for His teaching because He ministered to them. Women with all sorts of diseases — mental, spiritual, and physical — came to Jesus and were healed.

Jesus was a man of action. He didn't only talk about God: He did the work of God on earth. When He ordered demons to leave, they left. When He rebuked a fever, it fled. When He spoke life to the dead, they lived.

Apparently, Jesus didn't always feed 5,000, the Twelve, and Himself with a little boy's lunch. According to Scripture, financially independent women supported Jesus' ministry and helped foot the bill.

Keep these women contributors in mind whenever you read the life of Jesus as recorded in the Gospels. Their position as financial supporters of Jesus' ministry is very interesting, especially in relationship to Judas, the disciple whom Jesus entrusted to manage the finances for the Twelve. Contributing women disciples would have dealt with Judas on a regular basis as he felt free to criticize offerings that didn't pass through his sticky fingers. (Jn. 12:4-6)

And you probably know where Judas was at the crucifixion of Jesus — dead and buried (Mt. 27:1-10). Although the movement the women disciples financially supported seemed to be falling apart, they were there at the cross (Mk. 15:40-1).

Was Dorcas/Tabitha among these women at the crucifixion? Did she stand at the foot of the cross? Had Jesus cast a demon out of her? Or healed her from a disease? Was she wealthy?

For many questions, there is no answer: however, we will get an answer of sorts to that last question.

Problems and Great Possibilities with Widows

God has a decidedly soft spot for widows and orphans. Not surprisingly, so did the fledgling early church.

In the first century, the social safety net was torn. Married women received a dowry, which was often all that stood between them and starvation if they should be widowed (Lk. 15:7-9). Beyond that, begging or prostitution were often their only career opportunities.

Rather than ignoring the poor, the early Church took Jesus' teaching to heart and developed a novel approach to the poor in their midst. The first Church committee ever appointed and organized, after the twelve disciples, was for the purpose of caring for widows. While this method of church growth is often neglected today, the Scripture tells us that ministry to the widows had a dramatic effect. The word of God spread and the number of disciples in Jerusalem increased rapidly. Surprisingly a large number of priests became obedient to the faith. (Acts 6:7, NIV)

I like to imagine that in Jaffa on the Mediterranean Coast, the entire widow's benevolence committee was the responsibility of one woman named Dorcas/Tabitha.

Anywhere men go down to the sea in boats, along with the tang of salt in the air, there will be widows and orphans. These are the human wreckage washed up by ill tides. Ancient Jaffa had its share of human flotsam.

While the poverty-stricken may not be the target demographic of some church planners, they were Dorcas' people. As the cold winter rains blew in off the sea, the church in Jaffa was being built one stitch at a time.

How important was Dorcas/Tabitha's ministry? She was not a preacher or a teacher but there is that moment in an upstairs chamber that revealed the value of Dorcas/Tabitha's gifts. And what a surprising value it was.

Sown in the Spirit

What would happen when Peter sought the face of the Almighty on behalf of this woman who was so filled with the goodness of God? The crowd questioned each other as they silently filed out of the room. They all agreed on one thing: Unexplainable power accompanied Peter and other disciples:

The Holy Spirit fell on believers when Peter and John prayed. (Acts 8)

Saul, the main persecutor of the Christians, had been blinded and then healed. Now he was a Christian, too. (Acts 9:1-19)

In Lydda, not too far from Jaffa, Peter had been the instrument of healing for Aeneas, a paralytic of eight years. (Acts 9:32-35) What might God do through him today?

Silence fell over the crowd as they strained their ears and imaginations. What sort of transaction was passing between the upper chamber and the throne room of God?

Then they heard Peter's commanding voice shout, "Dorcas, arise!"

Seconds later, laughter emanated from the upper chamber, punctuated by shouts of praise.

Peter appeared at the doorway. "Come and see what the Lord has done!" he invited.

Slowly, fearfully, uncertain of what they would see, the people climbed up the stairs. Some could not believe their eyes.

There, on the edge of her bier, sat Dorcas, alive, well, and smiling.

And she still lives on!

Following the Thread

Dorcas and her work still live, thanks to a church in the very shadow of the house of Simon the tanner.

Most tourists will not find this church by themselves. Tucked down a winding alleyway and built on landlocked ancient foundations, this spectacularly beautiful Eastern Orthodox church was scorched by fire many years ago. Restored, its murals gleam today with pristine beauty. But like all functioning churches, the real story is not in the beauty of its windows and furnishings but in the spiritual life of its congregation. And this little church shines with a rare beauty beyond antiquities and treasures.

The church's congregation is admittedly poor in gold and earthly treasures. Its members are largely comprised of the faithful swept in during the Russian immigration or low-paid foreign domestics and caretakers of the elderly working in Israel on work visas. But, says their shepherd, a joyful, dark-eyed man, they are eager for the Word. As proof, the three services held weekly in Russian, Romanian, and Serbo-Croatian are standing room only.

"We consider Dorcas the mother of our church," he said.

(Remember, I promised earlier to provide proof.)

Then he told me the oral legends of Dorcas passed down through the years. "She was a talented woman made wealthy from her craft as a seamstress," he said. "She followed Jesus as His disciple and never married. Her life was poured out to build His church by helping the poor."

The church Dorcas founded remembers her by collecting good used clothes, washing and repairing them, and distributing them to the needy. It is a matter of the poor helping the poorer.

Although Israel boasts of a rising middle class and a good standard of living, there are still those who need help for one reason or another. One doesn't have to go far to see who the needy are. On the street corner amid traffic stands an elderly skinny Anglo, cup-in-hand, gravely asking for help. Many of the needy are elderly who came to Israel during the Russian immigration and don't speak Hebrew. They are finding it hard to make a living in a young country where charities are few.

But the church in Jaffa, led by the example of Dorcas, is being built one stitch at a time. Following the example of the faithful disciple who lived so long ago, they continue to do what they can to clothe the naked as if they were clothing Christ Himself (Mt. 25).

Want to do something of lasting value? Want to do something that will stretch into eternal value? Do something for the least important, least influential, the least of the least. Jesus will consider it as much a personal favor as if you did it for Him.

Let's Talk About Dorcas
A. According to the story of Dorcas, what kind of deeds have long-lasting effects upon the world?
B. If Dorcas lived today, what do you think she would be involved with?
C. The sky's the limit! What would you like to do to help others in need?

What can you do?

D. Jesus said, "I tell you the truth, whatever you did for one of the least of these brothers of mine, you did for me." (Mt. 25:40) Why do you think Jesus closely identifies with the poor? Why do you think Jesus wants us to care for those less fortunate? What does He expect us to do for the poor whose misfortune is their own fault?

E. Many times, as in Dorcas' church in modern Jaffa, the poor are the most generous. How do you think God will judge the wealthy who are stingy?

F. What do you admire most about Dorcas? How could you become more like her?

Just Between You and God

Ask God to bring someone needy across your path whom you can help.

Notes for Facilitators

Thank you for choosing *Ancient Secrets of Ten Bible Women* for your Bible study. I realize there are a lot of Bible studies, and I appreciate you choosing this one.

I want to personally pray for you that the Holy Spirit helps you to adapt this Bible study to the spiritually hungry women and men who attend. If you want prayer support, please send me an email marked Attention Rebekah at info@rebekah.org. I have an active Facebook prayer team at Rebekah Binkley Montgomery Author who will also pray for you and those attending your study. Perhaps you would like to join us in praying for other facilitators and study groups.

The Narrative
Did you ever read a children's Bible storybook? The narrative makes the story more understandable, relevant, and memorable.

While sticking closely to the scripture, this study has a strong narrative component for the same reason. Essentially, the study is Bible stories written for adults.

To better explain the time, culture, lifestyle, religious practices, each woman profiled has a contemporary example. As examples: We meet the two Bedouin sisters in Chapter One. In Chapter Two, we learn a little about modern Bethlehem and its weather before time-traveling to ancient Bethlehem known by Naomi and Ruth.

Life Application
The key to a memorable Bible study was given to me by an old preacher: You tell them what you are going to tell them. Then you tell them. And then you tell them what you told them. One life-changing, God-inspired thought, hammered securely into the heart and mind of the participant is the goal.

That preacher had a lot of wisdom. I have tried to follow his advice with the structure of *Ancient Secrets of Ten Bible Women*:

At the beginning of each study, we tell them what we are going to tell them: "In this study we will learn —"

The teaching portion of each study will "tell them."

The "Let's talk about ..." section reiterates what we told them.

"Just between you and God" nails the lesson home so participants might hide it in their hearts.

Group Size

Ancient Secrets of Ten Bible Women is designed to be flexible, adapting to your group's size and goals.

Personal study: You may choose to use this for a personal Bible study guide. If you ask, the Holy Spirit will meet with you and illuminate the lessons. I encourage you to look up the Bible references.

Small group study: In beta testing, small group Bible study participants couldn't wait until the end of each chapter to share their thoughts. For that reason, I have placed notations marking "Let's talk about ..." discussion starters throughout each chapter. Look for alphabet letters in parentheses. (A) references the (A) question in the "Let's talk about ..." section at the end of each chapter, and so on.

I encourage you to briefly review the previous lesson before you introduce the chapter of the week, since each lesson builds on the previous one.

Suggest your participants read the lesson ahead of coming to a Bible study group to discuss it. When you meet, assume they haven't read it. You may want to ask for volunteers to read a section at a time. Also, you might hand out the Bible verses that are marked (Read ...) with the reference so they can be read when they appear in the narrative.

Each Bible study group is as unique as the women involved. Do what fits your participants' needs. Share your ideas on the *AncientSecrets.com* website.

Large group study: *Ancient Secrets* was first beta tested before a Bible study group of approximately 125 women seated at tables in the church's atrium. Each table had a hostess, and the women took turns bringing a dessert or snack. A fair-sized proportion of the participants were unchurched, knowing little about the Bible.

Some large groups have presented the studies like a radio show with a variety of women voicing the characters in the story. I'll use the chapter on Deborah as an example of how the studies can be presented.

Announcer 1: No doubt about it: Deborah the prophetess makes some nervous.

Why? Perhaps because she doesn't fit the stereotypical demure-little-woman mold. Or perhaps because Deborah was courageous, and her courage strikes terror and conviction in the fainthearted. Maybe because her God-given prophetic vision saw people as they truly were.

Or perhaps because Deborah—whose name means "bee"—personified her fierce but valuable little namesake with sweetness for her people and a sting for their enemies.

Or maybe it was because she goaded the terrified into facing the object of their fear. That's what Deborah did. She inspired a fainthearted leader and his nervous army to face impossible odds in the name of the Lord.

Whatever the reason, she packed a punch in her day. She still does.

We know only snippets of Deborah's private life. For example, her husband's name was Lappidoth (which means "a light") and she felt called to be a mother to Israel. Jews the world over consider her a mother to their race, nation, and religion.

Why does this motherly woman cause nervousness after thousands of years? Is it because she knew how to motivate people to do the right thing despite their fears?

We'll find out as we look at Deborah the prophetess and the battle she helped win.

Announcer 2:
In this study we will learn how to:
✓ ask and receive godly wisdom for your battles.
✓ recognize God's leading.
✓ motivate someone who knows what God wants but is reluctant to follow God's direction.

From the summit of Mount Tabor, a blazing sunset stretches over the Jezreel Valley. Below, the River Kishon (its name means "winding") winks reflected light as it twists through the valley.

Most of the year, the Kishon seems tame. Don't be fooled. Let a cloudburst take place in the faraway western mountains and meek little Kishon becomes a raging torrent. Remember this. It's an important clue to Deborah's victory.

In the twilight, Gabrielle, a former captain of the Israeli army and someone met on a past trip to Israel, surveys the valley for defensive and offensive positions.

Gabrielle: The Jezreel Valley (also known as the Valley of Armageddon) is a perfect battleground. King Saul and his sons and King Josiah all died in battles here. Gideon fought and defeated the Midianites here. The final battle in Revelation will be fought here. And of course, Deborah and Barak fought here.

The earth is porous around the Kishon. It soaks up and holds

101

moisture. Long ago, when the river flooded, it became a quagmire. Today, we have better, more sophisticated ways of managing water. While most Israeli women serve in the army, they do not serve in combat positions. The sheer physical strain of battle is considered too much for women. In shoulder-to-shoulder fighting with male soldiers, it is thought that men would take risks to protect the women.

Announcer 1: How would men fight if they had only one woman to protect? And what if they saw that lone woman as their mother?

Announcer 2: A Date Under the Palm between Ramah and Bethel, Between 1209 BC and 1169 BC
Wind rippled the palm fronds above Deborah and blew up skiffs of dust.
Deborah: *A change in the weather is coming. The dry season will soon end.*

Announcer 2: This day Deborah would decide legal matters for the people of the land. Families with disputes, neighbors with property questions, parents with unruly children, accused thieves, widows cheated out of their inheritance — the line of people waiting for her words of wisdom snaked behind the palm and circled around.
Deborah: *Oh Lord, I need Your wisdom and words.*

Announcer 2: She only needed to ask. And listen.

Announcer 1: A Galilean farmer stepped forward to present his case.

Farmer: Mother Deborah, many times our village has been pillaged by Sisera's army. They steal our crops. They take our sons and daughters as slaves. On the high places they worship Baal. Is there no God in Israel?

Deborah: What is your tribe?

Farmer: Naphtali.

You get the idea. It takes some practice for the transitions to be seamless. Some of the names are tongue-twisters and require practice. But it is a great way to present the studies. It gets people involved and hammers down the lesson of each study.
The following is a listing of the goals for each chapter along with questions corresponding to the letters in each chapter.

Chapter One
Rahab the Harlot: Survivor? Or Traitor?

In this study we will learn:
✓ how God sends warnings before visiting judgement.
✓ when to act in a crisis.
✓ how to face your fears and conquer them.

Let's Talk About Rahab
A. Rahab foresaw Jericho's destruction and acted when she had the opportunity. What do you see that is threatening to destroy our nation? Churches? Individuals? Families? Yourself? What steps can you take to diminish those threats?
B. God revealed His power and nature to Rahab prior to the spies' arrival. Where have you experienced God's presence?
C. Why do you think Rahab chose to make a pact with the spies rather than betray them and perhaps save Jericho?
D. There were likely many prostitutes in Jericho. Why do you think God chose Rahab to offer hospitality to the spies?
E. Do you think Rahab was a traitor to the people of Jericho? A realist? Or something else?
F. Rahab made a pact with the spies to save her life and that of her family members. What steps can we take to protect our families from destructive influences both inside the home and from outside?
G. Do you think God still warns people of coming judgement? Have you ever been warned by God to avoid someone or something?
H. The author sees the red cord as symbolic of the blood of Jesus that buys our salvation. What, if anything, do you see the red cord as symbolizing?

Just Between You and God:
Tell God about situations you feel threaten your faith, family, community, etc. Ask Him what—if anything—He wants you to do to address the threat.

Chapter Two
Ruth and Naomi: Love Makes a Dream Come True

In this study we will learn:
✓ the principle of "deeds are seeds."
✓ a pattern for committed love.
✓ how to thrive in a crisis.

103

Let's Talk About Ruth and Naomi
A. Who was your spiritual mentor? Tell us what she/he did to help you grow spiritually?
B. Have you ever acted as a spiritual mentor to another? Tell us about your experience. Was it rewarding? Disappointing? Difficult?
C. The Bible says, "You reap what you sow" twenty-eight times with slightly different wording but they nearly all mean the same thing. Some examples are Galatians 6:7 , 2 Corinthians 9:6, and Psalm 126:5, all wording from the NIV. Have you ever seen or experienced evidence of the "deeds are seeds" concept?
D. Read Ruth's pledge to Naomi in Ruth 1:16-17. How would you describe someone who inspires this much loyalty?
E. We know of parents adopting children, but rarely of children adopting parents as Ruth did Naomi. What reasons do you think someone would have for turning their back on their life, family, country, and gods to adopt another way of life?
F. What types of relationships foster a closer walk with God? What types of relationships causes people to wander away from Him?

Just Between You and God
Read 2 Corinthians 12: 7b-10.

Ask God: Are there any relationships You want to me to give up to grow closer to You?

Chapter Three
Deborah the Prophetess: How Her Strategy Won a War

In this study we will learn how to:
✓ ask and receive godly wisdom for your battles.
✓ recognize God's leading.
✓ motivate the someone who knows what God wants but is reluctant to follow God's direction.

Let's Talk About Deborah
A. How do you feel about women leaders? Why do you think strong women like Deborah sometimes make some nervous?
B. What kind of person does it take to arbitrate legal matters and give sage personal advice? To whom do you look for sound advice?
C. Why do you think Barak was afraid to go to battle without Deborah?
D. Imagine you are a modern-day Deborah. What great evil in the world would you fight? What would you do? What can you do?
E. What qualities of Deborah's would you like to emulate?

Just Between You and God

God, You called me to stand against evil in the world. What should I do and how shall I do it?

Chapter Four
Bathsheba: Temptress or Victim?
In this study we will answer these questions:

✓ Can a marriage that starts out wrong ever be right?
✓ Can a reputation damaged by scandal ever be repaired? Or will people always remember the sin?

Let's talk about Bathsheba

A. When a marriage or life begins on the wrong foot, how can God help it get back on track?
B. Uriah, Bathsheba's first husband, appears to be a loving, honorable man and soldier, devoted to his wife. David had fame, riches, and several wives. Why do you think some women find wealth, power, fame, and talent more desirable than committed love?
C. The author's opinion is that Bathsheba could have said no to David's advances but chose not to. What's yours? Could Bathsheba have said no?
D. How does following godly wisdom help repair a damaged reputation?
E. Has this study changed your perception of Bathsheba? Why and how? Or not.

Just Between You and God

Do you have a failure that has affected your life in negative ways? Ask God how He can help you turn it into a blessing for you and others.

Chapter Five
The Wise Woman of Tekoah: She Used Her Talent to Heal a Family and Nation

In this study we will learn that:

✓ God gives each of us various talents and gifts
✓ no matter how average or unremarkable our talent, He can use it to further His purposes.
✓ the biblical definition of wisdom is knowing what season it is.

Let's Talk About the Wise Woman of Tekoah —

A. David felt unable to pronounce judgment on his son Absalom for killing his brother because of his own sin in arranging the death of Bathsheba's husband along with his men. What kind of actions or situations can cause a parent to lose moral authority?

B. How do you think David should have responded to his daughter's rape by her brother? What punishment fits the crime?

C. Absalom waited for David to do something. When he didn't, Absalom took revenge by killing his brother. Is vigilante justice ever warranted?

D. Sometimes a person is too close to a problem to properly address it. What can you do to help someone gain perspective on their situation?

E. What characteristics do you look for in a wise person?

Just Between You and God

Ask God how to wisely use the talent or gifts He has given you. Ask Him what steps you should take to maximize it to fulfill His purpose for loaning it to you.

Chapter Six
The Widow of Zarephath: She Fed Her Family on Faith

In this study we will learn:
✓ how to hear and discern God's voice.
✓ what God expects when He gives us a talent.
✓ trusting and obeying God is often counter-intuitive.
✓ there is a reward for those who trust Him.

Let's Talk About the Widow

A. Although Nediva was not a Jewess, God asked her to exercise great faith. Share your story of how you came to faith in Jesus.

B. Do you think God still speaks? Can you tell of a time you "heard" God's voice?

C. Baal demanded the sacrifice of infants and children to bring prosperity. Today, babies are routinely slaughtered in the womb for a variety of reasons, one of which is for economic advancement. What would you say to a woman contemplating an abortion?

D. What type of cruel false gods do you see worshipped today?

E. God did a miracle for Nediva and fed her during a famine. Has God ever provided for you in a miraculous way? Share your story.

F. Jesus found Nediva's faith to be remarkable. What do you find outstanding about her?

Just Between You and God
Is there something in your past that haunts you? Do you need to make restitution for something you have done? Ask God to lead you to scripture verses that pertain to your past situation.

Chapter Seven
Mary of Nazareth: What Did it Cost Her to be God's Handmaiden?

In this study we will learn:
✓ you were not born by accident.
✓ God has a purpose for you.
✓ what it truly means to invite Jesus to live in us.
✓ it may cost us to be a follower of Jesus.

Let's Talk About Mary
A. How do you think you would react if your thirteen-year-old daughter made a similar announcement?
B. What is your opinion of ancient writings about Mary that are not included in the canonical Bible? Should they be accepted as truth? Or should the canonical Bible be the sole authority on Mary's life
C. How do you think you would react if you met an angel face-to-face? What questions would you ask the angel if you were asked to carry God's own Son?
D. What clues to Mary's character and personality do you find in The Magnificat?
E. What lines from The Magnificat speak to you?
F. The Holy Spirit that placed the Seed of God in Mary's womb is the same Holy Spirit that places the Seed of God in your heart. As pregnancy changes the shape of a woman, so are our lives changed. What changes have you experienced if you have said, "Be it unto me as you have said"?

Just Between You and God
Has God ever spoken to you about doing something out-of-the-ordinary for Him? What is your response to Him?

Chapter Eight
Anna the Prophetess: What Was Her Vision for Tomorrow?

In this study we will learn:
✓ about effective spiritual disciplines.
✓ some of the ways those disciplines can be exercised.
✓ Satan will oppose you if you practice the disciplines.

Let's Talk About Anna
A. Some people see the future as bleak. How do you see the future? Rosy? Dark? Why?
B. What would you like to see the future bring to your children and grandchildren?
C. What good things could you be praying that the future will bring? How could your prayers be turned into actions on your part?
D. Have you ever fasted? Why do you think God calls people to fast?
E. When Anna and Simeon saw the Baby Jesus, they believed that although Israel was under Rome, their people had a future. According to their words, what do you think they expected the Messiah to do?
F. If you could ask God for a blessing for the future of your family, town, state, and country, what would it be?

Just Between You and God
Since He expects us to fast, ask God what sort of fast He wants you to follow.

Chapter Nine
The Woman at the Well: Why Did Jesus Go Out of His Way to Ask Her for A Drink?

In this study we will learn:
✓ what living water is.
✓ the kind of worship God desires from us.
✓ where to find true satisfaction with life.

Let's Talk About the Woman at the Well
A. Women semi-seriously joke about "loving chocolate." Why do you think many women turn to chocolate or another type of food for happiness or comfort?
B. What do you observe women doing to alleviate stress, sadness, disappointment, rejection, boredom, etc.?
C. What do you think women who have multiple intimate relationships are searching for?
D. Because of her immoral behavior, her community shunned Umnia. How

should we treat people whose lifestyles we disapprove of?

E. Do you think Jesus went out of His way to talk to Umnia? Why or why not?

F. Although Umnia had a checkered past, why do you think her past was not an obstacle to Jesus?

G. What do you think Jesus was offering Umnia?

H. What does the term "living water" mean to you?

Just between you and God:
What yearnings does God wish to satisfy in you?

Chapter Ten
Dorcas: She Built a Church with a Needle

In this study we will learn:
✓ how women disciples contributed to Jesus's ministry.
✓ what Dorcas/Tabitha was doing in Joppa.
✓ what happened to the church she started
✓ what matters to Jesus.

Let's talk about Dorcas
According to the story of Dorcas, what kind of deeds have long-lasting effects upon the world
What do you admire most about Dorcas? How could you become more like her?

A. The sky's the limit! What would you like to do to help others in need? What can you do?

Just Between You and God
Ask God to bring someone needy across your path whom you can help.

ABOUT THE AUTHOR

Rebekah Binkley Montgomery began her writing career in grade school writing poetry for a church newsletter. "If my father wasn't the pastor, my poems wouldn't have seen ink. It gave me the writing bug." In high school, she wrote stories for Primary Days (Scripture Press), a Sunday school paper.

From 1972-1984, she was on staff of several evangelical churches writing illustrated sermons, plays, musicals, devotionals, teaching materials, and articles. As a freelance writer, she was senior editor of six craft and special interest publications while managing a support staff. She produced thirty-eight issues a year, plus one-shot specials, books, calendars, and other items. In the areas of nostalgia and collectibles, the titles under her editorship achieved the highest circulation in their genre. She was a well-known speaker for women's retreats, conferences, children's camps, and Bible schools both in the states and internationally.

Rebekah also hosted a satellite collector's show for Shop At Home network (Knoxville, TN) for two years. She has served as pastor of a country church, children's pastor, pulpit fill, interim pastor, associate pastor, and women's and children's pastor.

Rebekah attended Christian Training Center, Fort Wayne, Fort Wayne Bible College, Institute of Fine Arts, IU-Purdue, Fort Wayne campus, American Institute of Holy Land Studies, and Jerusalem University College, Jerusalem. Her course of studies included Bible history and exegesis, and literature. She was on the Board of Directors of Right to the Heart, co-publisher of Jubilant Press, and was twice sponsored by the Israeli Ministry of Tourism as a visiting journalist. She also attended post-graduate classes in Israel.

Business and Professional Women named her a 2009 Woman of the Year. She was the 2010 recipient of the Beyond Me award for service.

In 2003, she contracted West Nile encephalitis from an infected mosquito resulting in right side paralysis. She taught herself to function left-handed, eventually regaining most of her righthanded skill. She was diagnosed in 2016 with viral parkinsonism. She continued to speak and teach until creeping disability robbed her of reliable speech. Today, sometimes she can talk: sometimes she can't. Her sister Ruth Binkley Whatley acts as her stand-in voice.

Ancient Secrets of Ten Bible Women is her 10th published book. Other titles include the *Harvest of...* series, and *Ordinary Miracles* (Promise Press); *Faithprints: Touching Your World for Jesus* (Leafwood), and her first novel *Hunt the Straight Path Home* (Abundance Books) for which she was awarded Historical Novel of the Year by Advanced Writers and Speakers Association. She estimates she has written over 1000 articles.

She lives in Decatur, Indiana, with John her husband of fifty-three years and Steve, their cat. She has three grown children and two grandchildren.

Her webpage is rebekahmontgomery.com

Email address: info@rebekah.org

Find her on Facebook at RebekahBinkleyMontgomery

THANK YOU!

Thank you for reading this book from Mt. Zion Ridge Press.

If you enjoyed the experience, learned something, gained a new perspective, or made new friends through story, could you do us a favor and write a review on Goodreads or wherever you bought the book?

Thanks! We and our authors appreciate it.

We invite you to visit our website, *MtZionRidgePress.com*, and explore other titles in fiction and non-fiction. We always have something coming up that's new and off the beaten path.

And please check out our podcast, **Books on the Ridge,** where we chat with our authors and give them a chance to share what was in their hearts while they wrote their book, as well as fun anecdotes and glimpses into their lives and experiences and the writing process. And we always discuss a very important topic: *Tea!*

You can listen to the podcast on our website or find it at most of the usual places where podcasts are available online. Please subscribe so you don't miss a single episode!

Thanks for reading. We hope you come back soon!

www.ingramcontent.com/pod-product-compliance
Lightning Source LLC
Chambersburg PA
CBHW011223120626
46545CB00010B/3126